SOCIAL EATS

A big thank you to everyone who's ever eaten at any of my pop-ups or events, to those who've worked with me to get to where I am today, and particularly to my parents, Papa G and Yvonne, my sisters, the amazing Naomi, for putting up with my workaholic nature, and my mates for keeping my feet firmly on the ground!

First published in Great Britain in 2015 by
Kyle Books, an imprint of Kyle Cathie Ltd.
192–198 Vauxhall Bridge Road
London SW1V 1DX
general.enquiries@kylebooks.com
www.kylebooks.com

10 9 8 7 6 5 4 3 2 1

ISBN 978 0 85783 279 5

Editor **Judith Hannam**
Editorial Assistant **Hannah Coughlin**
Designer **Helen Bratby**
Photographer **Clare Winfield**
Prop Stylis **Iris Bromet**
Food Stylist **Rosie Reynolds**
Production **Gemma John** and **Nic Jones**

A Cataloguing in Publication record for this title is available from the British Library.

Colour reproduction by ALTA London.
Printed and bound in Singapore by Tien Wah Press

JIMMY GARCIA

SOCIAL EATS

FOOD TO IMPRESS YOUR MATES

PHOTOGRAPHY BY CLAIRE WINFIELD

CONTENTS

HI THERE!

Thanks so much for buying my book. I hope you get as much pleasure out of making the dishes as I have in creating them.

To me, food is the best way to bring people together – and an opportunity to have fun, which is what I'm all about!

I've been fortunate enough to be able to turn my passion into my profession. I began cooking with my Spanish father at a very early age, and as a teenager worked as a part-time commis. My journey to self-taught chef really began, however, when I did a ski season as a chalet host in the French Alps, cooking for 12 guests as a 19 year old, prior to going to university. I then worked as a private chef on a super yacht in the Mediterranean every summer. With a limitless budget, amazing ingredients, and demanding guests, I quickly developed my own style and dishes to impress.

On the back of this experience, I decided to turn my front room into a restaurant one evening a month, borrowing the tables and chairs from a local church. I put scrolls through my neighbours' doors, my housemates did the waitering, and I was on my way. It was fantastic! The buzz – diners staying until 4am, drinking and dancing on the tables – had me completely hooked. The only downside was that I had to have the tables and chairs back at the church by 9am the following morning, and then was obliged to go to the service. Don't get me wrong. I'm not against going to church at all, quite the contrary, but on three hours' sleep it was a tough one.

I soon became obsessed with finding weird and wonderful venues at which to hold dining experiences: wine shops, warehouses, hairdressers, roof terraces . . . we even put a kitchen in a bedroom once for a surprise wedding – a long story! It soon became clear that what had started out as a bit of fun was taking off, as we had sell-out nights and great press reviews. Within a year I'd moved to France for the winter to set up a catered chalet company called Ski Bluebird, and to launch my pop-up restaurants in the Alps before coming back to the UK for the summer and launching big pop-up projects alongside an outside catering company.

This book is a collection of my favourite dishes from my various experiences over the past few years, whether cooking in chalets, at weddings, events and pop-ups, or with my father and friends.

I cook to make people happy as it makes me happy. Simple. None of the dishes in here are rocket science . . . they are fun, creative and delicious. So get cooking and enjoy yourself! Turn the radio up, grab a beer and get into the swing!

AT THE PARTY

SMALL BITES & LITTLE DISHES

AVOCADO CREAM PROFITEROLES WITH SALMON RŒ

Profiteroles are super easy to make, and once they're done you can fill them with all sorts of sweet and savoury fillings – experiment! Makes 20

FOR THE CHOUX PASTRY
50G BUTTER, CUT INTO CUBES
50G STRONG PLAIN FLOUR, SIFTED
2 MEDIUM EGGS, BEATEN
SALT AND FRESHLY GROUND
  BLACK PEPPER

FOR THE AVOCADO CREAM
1 AVOCADO
100G CRÈME FRAÎCHE
JUICE OF 1 LEMON
20G SALMON ROE
20 BABY PEA SHOOTS

Preheat the oven to 200°C/gas mark 6. Line a baking tray with greaseproof paper and run it under a tap for a couple of seconds, then pour away any excess water – this helps generate more steam in the oven, which in turn will help the pastry to rise and make those fluffy profiteroles even fluffier!

To make the choux pastry, place 150ml water and the butter in a small pan over a medium heat. As soon as the butter is melted and the water comes up to the boil, turn off the heat, as you don't want too much water to evaporate. Add the flour and beat in with a whisk until you have a smooth ball of paste, then add the eggs and a touch of seasoning.

Spoon 20 teaspoons of the mix on to the tray or, for best results, use a piping bag fitted with a plain nozzle, leaving at least 2.5cm between each profiterole.

Bake in the oven for around 12 minutes, then increase the heat to 220°C/gas mark 7 for a further 15 minutes or until the profiteroles are golden and crispy. Remove from the oven, pierce the side of each one with a small skewer to let out the steam, place on a wire rack and allow to cool.

Place the avocado, crème fraîche and lemon juice in a food processor, blend until smooth, then spoon into a piping bag with a small nozzle.

Once the profiteroles have cooled, make a small hole in the base of each and fill with the avocado cream. Spoon on a small teaspoon of salmon roe and top with a baby pea shoot. These should be eaten within an hour and a half of filling, but for best results serve them straight away.

TUNA & SESAME LOLLIPOPS

These look great, taste great and are really simple to make. The only issue is that when cutting the tuna into perfect circles you're left with some trimmings – but these can be diced up and used for ceviche (see page 78). Makes 8

50G SESAME SEEDS
2 TUNA STEAKS, APPROXIMATELY
   150G EACH AND ABOUT
   1CM THICK
SESAME OIL
SALT AND FRESHLY GROUND
   BLACK PEPPER
COLA AND SOY REDUCTION
   (PAGE 77) OR AVOCADO CREAM
   (PAGE 40), FOR DIPPING

Preheat the oven to 180°C/gas mark 4.

Spread the sesame seeds on a baking tray lined with baking parchment, and toast in the oven for 10 minutes, or until lightly golden. Remove from the oven and allow to cool.

Meanwhile, using a 3-4cm round cutter or the rim of a shot glass, cut out 4 circles from each tuna steak. Place the trimmings in the fridge to use another time. Roll the outsides of the tuna circles in the sesame seeds to form a nice crust. Season.

Heat a griddle pan over a high heat with a small splash of oil then flash fry the tuna circles for around 30 seconds. Insert a lollipop stick through the middle of each, then serve with the dip of your choice.

These can be served hot or cold, but are best when hot and fresh.

CURRIED SWEET POTATO BLINIS WITH COURGETTE RIBBONS & TSATZIKI

In 2013, I was asked to cater for a wedding for a good friend of mine. The groom's family were Indian, and the bride's family were from Derbyshire, so we decided to do something that featured the best of both cultures! Makes about 16

FOR THE BLINIS
1 SWEET POTATO (ABOUT 150G),
   PEELED AND CHOPPED INTO
   1CM CUBES
50G BUTTER
2 MEDIUM EGGS
100ML WHOLE MILK
150G PLAIN FLOUR
1 TEASPOON BAKING POWDER
1 TEASPOON CURRY POWDER
1 TEASPOON GARAM MASALA
SALT AND FRESHLY GROUND
   BLACK PEPPER

FOR THE TSATZIKI
1 CUCUMBER, GRATED
200G GREEK YOGURT
BUNCH OF MINT, FINELY CHOPPED
JUICE OF 1 LEMON
1 GARLIC CLOVE, CRUSHED

FOR COURGETTE RIBBONS
2 COURGETTES, CUT INTO
   RIBBONS WITH A RIBBON PEELER

First make the blinis, place the sweet potato in a medium saucepan, cover with water, bring to the boil, and cook for around 15 minutes, or until completely soft. Drain the potato, add 30g of the butter, season with a pinch of salt and pepper, then blend using a hand-held electric blender.

Mix the eggs and the milk together in a large bowl, then stir in the sweet potato, followed by all the remaining dry ingredients, mixing well. The mixture should still be a little runny. If not, add a little more milk.

Heat a small frying pan over a medium heat and add a little of the remaining butter. Spoon small dollops of the mixture into the pan and cook for around 2 minutes on each side until golden. Transfer the cooked blinis to a plate lined with kitchen paper, to absorb any excess oil, and allow to cool. Repeat to use all the mixture.

Meanwhile, make the tsatziki. Wrap the grated cucumber tightly in a tea-towel to remove any excess moisture – this ensures the dip retains a nice, thick consistency and doesn't become overly watery. Place the Greek yogurt in a bowl, stir in the cucumber and add all the remaining ingredients.

Once the blinis are cooled, take a piece of courgette ribbon and lay it out flat on a work surface. Place a teaspoon of the tsatziki on the ribbon, then roll it up and place it on top of the blini – a tasty little morsel! Repeat to top all the blinis.

MINI GREEK SALADS IN BRIOCHE BASKETS

Another super quick, easy and light bite that's perfect for the 'salad bar crowd'. Makes 12

FOR THE BRIOCHE BASKETS
6 SLICES OF BRIOCHE BREAD,
  HALVED

FOR THE SALAD
40G FETA CHEESE, FINELY
  CHOPPED
1 TOMATO, FINELY DICED
10 GREEN OLIVES, PITTED AND
  FINELY DICED
¼ CUCUMBER, DESEEDED AND
  FINELY DICED
¼ RED ONION, FINELY SLICED
SPLASH OF OLIVE OIL
SPLASH OF BALSAMIC VINEGAR
PINCH OF SALT
MINT SPRIGS, TO GARNISH

Preheat the oven to 150°C/gas mark 2.

Roll out the bread slices using a rolling pin until super thin, then press them into 12 mini pastry cases. Bake for about 30 minutes until crispy and hard. And there you have it... brioche baskets! Allow to cool.

Combine the salad ingredients in a bowl. Spoon into the brioche baskets and garnish with a tiny sprig of mint.

Assemble just before serving to avoid the brioche going soggy.

DILL & LEMON CUPCAKES WITH SMOKED SALMON ICING

Not your standard cupcake! They can be served either as a canapé,
or as a lunchbox filler. Makes 12

FOR THE CUPCAKES
180G PLAIN FLOUR
1 TABLESPOON BAKING POWDER
2 MEDIUM EGGS
1 POT NATURAL YOGURT
5 TABLESPOONS VEGETABLE OIL
1 BUNCH DILL, FINELY CHOPPED
JUICE AND ZEST OF 1 LEMON

FOR THE ICING
150G SMOKED SALMON, PLUS
  EXTRA TO GARNISH
100G CRÈME FRAÎCHE
FRESHLY GROUND BLACK PEPPER
FRESH DILL, TO GARNISH

Preheat the oven to 160°C/gas mark 3. Line a large
12-hole muffin tin with paper muffin cases.

Sift the flour into a mixing bowl, then mix in all the
remaining cupcake ingredients with a whisk until fully
combined. Divide the mixture equally between the paper
cases. Bake for around 30 minutes, or until a skewer
inserted into the middle of a muffin comes out clean.
Cool on a wire rack.

Meanwhile, crack on with the icing. Place the salmon,
crème fraîche and black pepper in a food processor, and
blend to a smooth consistency. Spoon into a piping bag
fitted with a small star nozzle and pipe swirls on top of
the cakes. Garnish each cake with a flake of salmon and
a sprig of dill.

SMOKED SALMON, DILL & CREAM CHEESE ROULADES

These were a chalet-host special back in the day. Always a winner! Makes 12

2 TORTILLA WRAPS
50G CREAM CHEESE
150G SMOKED SALMON
1 BUNCH DILL, FINELY CHOPPED
ZEST AND JUICE OF ½ LEMON

Spread the tortillas with the cream cheese, then place a thin layer of smoked salmon on top. Sprinkle over the dill, lemon zest and juice, and wrap tightly into a roll. Wrap in clingfilm, twisting the ends to secure, then chill for 4 hours.

When ready to serve, remove the clingfilm and cut off the excess tortilla at the ends. Slice each wrap diagonally along the roll into 6 pieces, so they stand up in nice triangles.

CONFIT DUCK & BLUE CHEESE CROQUETTES

Most butchers sell ready-made confit duck legs, but for best results, and if you have the time (you'll need to start a day in advance), it's worth doing it yourself, but not for less than two legs. This recipe only needs one, so if you do make your own, reserve the second leg, shred it up and add it to a stir fry, or make some bangin' duck wraps for work the next day with a cheeky bit of cucumber and spring onion!
Serve with a relish of your choice – the Caramelised Onion Chutney always goes down a storm, as does the classic Orange and Earl Grey Chutney (see pages 78 and 61). Makes 12

FOR THE DUCK CONFIT (OPTIONAL)
2 DUCK LEGS
20G MALDON SEA SALT
20G BLACK PEPPERCORNS, CRUSHED
2 TABLESPOONS JUNIPER BERRIES
1 TABLESPOON CORIANDER SEEDS,
    CRUSHED
2 GARLIC CLOVES, CRUSHED
200G DUCK FAT OR 500ML VEG OIL
1 BAY LEAF
SPRIG OF FRESH THYME

FOR THE CROQUETTES
120G POTATOES (IDEALLY
    DESIREE), CHOPPED
20G BUTTER
1 CONFIT DUCK LEG
120G BLUE CHEESE (PREFERABLY
    A GOOD STILTON), CRUMBLED
100G PLAIN FLOUR
3 MEDIUM EGGS, LIGHTLY BEATEN
200G PANKO BREADCRUMBS
500ML VEG OIL FOR DEEP FRYING
SALT AND FRESHLY GROUND
    BLACK PEPPER

For the confit, if making, season the duck with the salt and pepper, then rub with the juniper berries, crushed coriander seeds and garlic. Place in the fridge overnight.

The next day, preheat the oven to 150°C/gas mark 2.

Pat the duck legs dry with kitchen paper, place in a small roasting tray with the duck fat or oil, add the bay leaf and thyme and cover with foil. Place in the oven and cook for about 2 hours or until the meat is falling off the bone. Remove the duck legs from the fat, place to one side to cool, then shred the meat from the bone.

For the croquettes, boil the potatoes until soft, then mash with the butter and some seasoning. Set aside to cool.

Divide the components of the croquettes – duck, potato, blue cheese – into 12 separate piles, then combine each so you have 12 piles of croquette filling. Using your hands, roll into cylindrical shapes, place on a tray and chill for 1 hour.

Once set, we need to pane them, which is just a posh word for breadcrumbing! Place the flour, egg and breadcrumbs into 3 separate shallow dishes. Roll the cylinders in flour, dip in the egg and then roll in the breadcrumbs. For a double pane, double whammy, dip the croquettes back into the egg, and then roll again in the breadcrumbs. This will help to produce an extra crispy 'jacket' for the croquettes.

Heat the oil in a deep pan to 160°C (check with a kitchen thermometer or see page 22) and deep-fry the croquettes, in batches of 4, for around 5 minutes until golden. Remove, using a slotted spoon, and place onto a plate lined with kitchen paper, to absorb any excess oil. Serve hot.

CRISPY PIG'S EARS WITH APPLE PURÉE DIP

This dish costs virtually nothing to make. Most butchers will give you the ears for free (but ask them to clean them for you and ensure there's no hair), and a couple of apples won't exactly break the bank. I cooked it on my live TV debut – trying to persuade Paul O'Grady to try pigs' ears was no easy task, but we got there in the end. Pigs' ears are very strongly flavoured, and may not be to everyone's taste, but they certainly do it for me! To make the Apple Purée Dip, see page 47 and add a teaspoon of ground cinnamon and nutmeg for a slightly spiced flavour. Serves 4

2 PIGS' EARS
3 SHALLOTS
2 CARROTS
2 LEEKS
2 BAY LEAVES
5 SPRIGS OF THYME
BLACK PEPPERCORNS
100G FLOUR
3 MEDIUM EGGS, LIGHTLY BEATEN
200G BREADCRUMBS
500ML OIL FOR DEEP FRYING
APPLE PURÉE DIP, TO SERVE
    (SEE PAGE 47)

Wash the ears, and place in a small pan of cold water. Bring to the boil and cook for 4 minutes. Remove from the heat.

In a medium pan, place the shallots, carrots, leeks, bay leaves, thyme sprigs, peppercorns, and add the ears. Cover with cold water, bring to the boil and then simmer on a medium–low heat for 2–3 hours, until a knife easily passes through them.

Once cooked, remove the ears from the pan with a slotted spoon and either discard the cooking liquid and vegetables, or freeze it and use to make a lovely, super-rich stock another time. Place the ears between 2 sheets of baking parchment with a weight on the top (to press down the ears) so we get nice neat strips! Set aside to cool.

Cut the ears into long strips. Place the flour, egg and breadcrumbs into 3 separate shallow dishes. Dip the strips in flour, dip in the egg and then roll in the breadcrumbs. Repeat and dip the strips back into the egg, and then roll again in the breadcrumbs.

Heat the oil in a deep pan to 180°C. If you don't have a kitchen thermometer, then to test the temperature place a small piece of breadcrumb in the oil and if it sizzles without burning straight away, it's ready. Deep-fry the coated strips in batches of 6 for around 4 minutes until golden and crispy. Remove, using a slotted spoon, and place onto a plate lined with kitchen paper, to absorb any excess oil.

Serve straight away with the Apple Purée Dip.

DUCK & ORANGE SALAD

This impressive starter is quite straightforward to do – it just requires a bit of planning. If you prefer, you can use normal breadcrumbs, but I think panko are the heavyweight pros when it comes to a crumb. Deep-frying the bon bons ensures that the foie gras in the middle becomes soft and releases all its flavour. Serves 4

FOR THE FOIE GRAS BON BONS
20ML VEGETABLE OIL
½ SHALLOT, FINELY DICED
1 GARLIC CLOVE, FINELY
    CHOPPED
120G MINCED DUCK BREAST
1 TEASPOON CHINESE FIVE
    SPICE POWDER
30G FOIE GRAS, CUT INTO 4
    CHUNKS (OPTIONAL)
50G PLAIN FLOUR
2 MEDIUM EGGS, LIGHTLY BEATEN
100G PANKO BREADCRUMBS
500ML VEGETABLE OIL FOR
    DEEP FRYING
SALT AND FRESHLY GROUND
    BLACK PEPPER

FOR THE DUCK SKIN
4 PIECES OF DUCK OR CHICKEN
    SKIN, ABOUT 8-10CM LONG
MALDON SEA SALT

FOR THE SMOKED DUCK BREAST
1 DUCK BREAST (AROUND 220G)
SALT AND FRESHLY GROUND
    BLACK PEPPER
500G WOOD CHIPPINGS
    (PREFERABLY MAPLE WOOD OR
    CLEMENTINE BARK AND LEAVES)

FOR THE SALAD
2 ORANGES, CUT INTO SEGMENTS
    (3 PER PERSON)
1 ENDIVE, LEAVES SEPARATED
    (2 PER PERSON)
1 COOKED BEETROOT, CUT INTO
    CHUNKS
SPOONFUL OF CHUTNEY

For the bon bons
Heat the vegetable oil in a medium frying pan and fry the shallots and garlic on a medium heat until softened, but not coloured.

Place the cooked garlic and onions in a mixing bowl and add the duck, five spice powder and salt and pepper. Combine well and then divide the mixture into 4 balls.

Using your thumb, press a piece of foie gras into the centre of each ball, if using, then cover it with the duck mixture. Place the flour, egg and breadcrumbs into 3 separate shallow dishes. Roll the balls in flour, dip in the egg and then roll in the breadcrumbs. For an extra crispy coating dip the balls back into the egg, and then roll again in the breadcrumbs.

Heat the oil in a deep pan to 160°C (check with a kitchen thermometer or see page 22) and deep-fry the balls, in batches of 6 for around 3 minutes until golden. Remove, using a slotted spoon, and place onto a plate lined with kitchen paper, to absorb any excess oil.

For the duck skin
Preheat the oven to 200°C/gas mark 6. Line a baking tray with baking parchment.

Prepare the skin by removing any excess fat (the gungy bit) – you should just be left with a very thin layer of outside skin. Lay each piece flat on the lined tray and generously season with salt. Place another layer of baking parchment on top, followed by another baking tray, and bake in the oven for 20–30 minutes, or until crispy and rigid. Leave the oven on to cook the duck breast. They will shrink a lot, but never fear, they'll taste incredible!

For the smoked duck breast
You can buy a ready-smoked duck breast for this salad but if you'd like to smoke the meat yourself, but don't have a smoker, I've got a renegade way to show you how to get some smoke into your meat. It's a great way to improvise!

Season the duck breast with salt and pepper. Line a small roasting tray with foil and then fill the base with wood chippings. Place a small grill rack above the chippings and rest the seasoned duck breast on top.

Light the chippings and, as soon as they start to burn, pour a splash of water into the bottom of the tray. Cover with foil, or a lid, and place on top of a gas or electric hob, on a high setting for 25 minutes and allow the smoke to infuse. After 25 minutes, remove the breast – the flesh should be a grey colour.

Fry the duck breast, with no oil, in a medium saucepan over a high heat, skin side down, for around 4 minutes, until golden brown. Seal the other side for 30 seconds before roasting in the oven at 200°C/gas mark 6 for 13 minutes.

Allow the breast to cool completely for about an hour before slicing really thinly on a diagonal.

To serve
Place a circle of chutney on each plate and top with a bon bon. Arrange the remaining salad ingredients with the thin slices of duck breast (4 per plate), before crushing the skin and to scatter over everything. Lovely stuff!

SCOTCH EGG SALAD

This is a bit of a champ! My good chef friend Eddie deserves some of the credit as he was the one who first came up with the idea of using finely chopped potato as a 'nest'. I decided to do a variation by creating a nest out of vegetable crisps and rocket. It not only looks great, but is a delight to eat too. When doing an event, we often place the nests in wicker baskets, and place the eggs on top. Serves 6

FOR THE SCOTCH EGGS

KNOB OF BUTTER
SPLASH OF TRUFFLE OIL
1 SHALLOT, FINELY DICED
1 GARLIC CLOVE
1 TABLESPOON DICED DRIED
   CRANBERRIES
1 TEASPOON FINELY CHOPPED
   SAGE
1 TEASPOON FINELY CHOPPED
   THYME
ZEST OF ½ ORANGE
150G PANKO BREADCRUMBS
1 TABLESPOON CRANBERRY
   JELLY OR JAM
150G SAUSAGE MEAT
6 QUAILS' EGGS
VEGETABLE OIL FOR DEEP FRYING
100G PLAIN FLOUR
3 EGGS, BEATEN
SALT AND FRESHLY GROUND
   BLACK PEPPER

FOR THE NEST

VEGETABLE OIL FOR DEEP FRYING
1 CARROT, CUT INTO RIBBONS
   WITH A RIBBON PEELER
1 PARSNIP, CUT INTO RIBBONS
   WITH A RIBBON PEELER
100G ROCKET

FOR THE DRESSING

25ML TRUFFLE OIL
15ML CIDER VINEGAR
1 TEASPOON CRANBERRY JELLY
   OR JAM

Place the butter and truffle oil in a medium frying pan, and fry the shallots and garlic until softened, then add the cranberries, sage, thyme, salt and pepper, orange zest and 1 tablespoon of the breadcrumbs.

Once the crumbs are golden, remove from the heat and add the cranberry jelly or jam. Allow to cool before mixing in the sausage meat.

Meanwhile, place the quails' eggs in a small pan of boiling water for 1 minute 50 seconds (for a runny centre). Drain and immediately put into a tub of iced water. This will shock them, and make life much easier when it comes to peeling.

Once the quails' eggs are peeled, carefully encase them in the sausage and herb mix. The best way to do this is to spread one-sixth of the sausage mix flat across the palm of one hand and then place the quail egg in the middle before folding the sides round. Be careful not to crush the eggs! It's a bit of a faff, but goes down a treat. Place in the fridge again to set, and crack on with the nest.

Heat the oil in a large deep pan to 160°C (check with a kitchen thermometer or see page 22) and deep-fry the ribbons, in 2 batches. Until they start to colour slightly. Remove and drain on kitchen paper. Once cooled, they should crisp up, giving a lovely vibrant colour!

Place the flour, egg and breadcrumbs into 3 separate shallow dishes. Dip the porky quails' eggs in flour, dip in the egg and then roll in the breadcrumbs. For an extra crispy coating dip the balls back into the egg, and then roll again in the breadcrumbs.

Reheat the oil in the deep pan to 160°C (check with a kitchen thermometer or see page 22) and deep-fry the coated porky eggs for around 5 minutes until lightly golden. Remove, using a slotted spoon, and place onto a plate lined with kitchen paper, to absorb any excess oil.

For the nest, place the rocket in a wicker basket, and add the veg crisps on top, before sporadically placing the eggs around the 'salad nest'.

Whisk together the oil, vinegar and jelly or jam, and drizzle over.

The true test is if the egg yolks are still runny. Are they?!

BEETROOT, CARAMELISED ONION & GOAT'S CHEESE TARTE TATINS

These tasty little morsels are a lovely winter quick-fix canapé. Makes 12

30G BUTTER, PLUS EXTRA
   FOR GREASING
1 RED ONION, FINELY CHOPPED
2 TABLESPOONS BALSAMIC
   VINEGAR
2 TABLESPOONS MUSCOVADO
   BROWN SUGAR
12 DISCS COOKED BEETROOT,
   AROUND 5MM THICK
12 SLICES GOAT'S CHEESE
2 X 25CM SHEETS PUFF PASTRY
1 TABLESPOON FRESH THYME
   LEAVES
SALT AND FRESHLY GROUND
   BLACK PEPPER

Preheat the oven to 200°C/gas mark 6. Grease a 12-hole small muffin tray with butter.

Melt the butter in a frying pan over a medium heat, add the onion and cook until beginning to soften (around 4 minutes), then add the balsamic vinegar, sugar and seasoning, and stir until the liquid has all evaporated, leaving you with lovely caramelised onions that can be used for loads of dishes!

Place a disc of beetroot, a slice of goat's cheese, and a small teaspoon of caramelised onion in each muffin hole.

Using a pastry cutter, glass or mug, cut out 2cm circles from the pastry sheets. Place on top of the onion, tucking the edges around the filling, then bake in the oven for 15 minutes, or until risen and golden. As soon as you've removed from the oven, press the pastry down gently, then remove from the tray and allow to cool on a wire rack. Garnish with a sprinkle of fresh thyme.

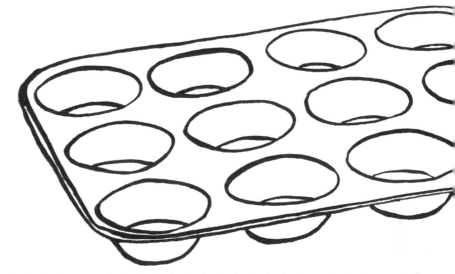

ULTIMATE CHICKEN DRUMMERS

Chicken drummers are great at the best of times, but this recipe's a banger! It takes some prep, but you won't be disappointed. I use chicken drumlets – where the small bone is taken off the breast of a chicken supreme – to make them look extra good and tasty! Serve with a chilli jam, or Red Onion Chutney (page 78) or simply with mayo... whatever your personal preference. Makes 12

12 CHICKEN DRUMLETS

FOR THE MARINADE
500ML BUTTERMILK
100ML SWEET CHILLI JAM
2 TABLESPOONS SALT

FOR THE CONFIT
500ML DUCK FAT OR
    VEGETABLE OIL
SPRIG OF THYME
2 GARLIC CLOVES, FINELY
    CHOPPED

FOR THE COATING
100G PLAIN FLOUR
1 TABLESPOON CAJUN SEASONING
1 TEASPOON DRIED CHILLI
    FLAKES
1 TABLESPOON DRIED OREGANO
3 MEDIUM EGGS, LIGHTLY BEATEN
150G PANKO BREADCRUMBS
VEGETABLE OIL FOR DEEP FRYING
SALT AND FRESHLY GROUND
    BLACK PEPPER

Clean the bone of each chicken drumlet, by scraping down it, so that all the meat gathers at the wider end of the cut of meat. Wrap foil around the bone to protect it during cooking and stop it from burning.

Place all the marinade ingredients in a non-metallic shallow dish, add the chicken, cover and marinate overnight in the fridge – this helps to tenderise them.

The next day, remove the chicken from the marinade and pat dry.

Preheat the oven to 130°C/gas mark 1.

Place the chicken and the confit ingredients in a roasting tin and bake in the oven for 3 hours or until the meat is falling off the bone – they'll be extremely fragile by now. Remove the chicken drumlets, and allow to cool.

Mix together the flour, spices and herbs and season well. Place the flour mixture, egg and breadcrumbs into 3 separate shallow dishes. Dip the drumlets in the flour mix, then in the egg, and then the breadcrumbs. Dip again into the egg and breadcrumbs. Remove the foil from the bones.

Heat the oil in a deep pan to 180°C (check with a kitchen thermometer or see page 22) and deep-fry the drumlets, in batches of about 6 for around 3 minutes, until golden. Remove, using a slotted spoon, and place onto a plate lined with kitchen paper to absorb any excess oil. Serve while hot.

MINTED LAMB LOLLIPOPS WITH MINT SAUCE DIP

These are basically just really well-trimmed lamb chops. Ask your butcher to trim them and clean the bone, giving your guests a handle to pick up the 'pops'. One of my clients nicknamed them lollipops and it's stuck ever since. Serves 8

8 TRIMMED LAMB CHOPS

FOR THE MARINADE
BUNCH OF MINT, LEAVES FINELY
  CHOPPED
2 GARLIC CLOVES, CRUSHED
40ML OLIVE OIL
2 SPRIGS OF ROSEMARY, LEAVES
  FINELY CHOPPED

FOR THE MINT SAUCE
BUNCH OF MINT, LEAVES FINELY
  CHOPPED
1 TABLESPOON GRANULATED
  BROWN SUGAR
3 TABLESPOONS CIDER VINEGAR
SALT AND FRESHLY GROUND
  BLACK PEPPER

Place the lamb chops in a shallow, non-metallic dish. Combine the marinade ingredients in a small jug, stir well and pour over the lamb. Season with a pinch of salt and pepper, then cover and place in the fridge overnight to marinate.

Next day, make the lovely tangy mint sauce for dipping. Place the chopped mint in a small bowl, and add 2 tablespoons boiling water, before adding the sugar and vinegar. Allow the mix to infuse, add some seasoning, and then add a wee bit more vinegar if you like it on the sharp side!

To cook the lamb chops, pop them on the preheated barbie for around 6 minutes on each side to serve them pink (just how I like them!). If you prefer the lamb cooked more, then leave on the barbie for up to another 3 minutes on each side. Set aside to rest for 5 minutes before serving with the mint sauce, for dipping.

MONKFISH NUGGETS WITH TARTARE SAUCE & TRIPLE-COOKED CHIPS

I love fish and chips and this is basically posh fish and chips. I went to university in Newcastle, and whenever we got the chance we used to drive out to the coast to Tynemouth, to a cracking little chippy, renowned for their golden batter. Eventually they told me their secret – turmeric! Serves 4

FOR THE TARTARE SAUCE
100G CUCUMBER, GRATED
1 TABLESPOON CORNICHONS,
    FINELY DICED
1 BUNCH PARSLEY, FINELY DICED
150G CRÈME FRAÎCHE (TASTIER
    THAN MAYO IN MY OPINION
    ON THIS ONE!)
1 TABLESPOON CAPERS
JUICE OF 1 LEMON
SALT AND FRESHLY GROUND
    BLACK PEPPER

FOR THE BATTER AND FISH
75G PLAIN FLOUR
75G CORNFLOUR
1 TEASPOON BAKING POWDER
1 TABLESPOON GROUND TURMERIC
75ML LAGER (A NICE BLOND BEER
    IS ALWAYS GOOD)
75ML SODA WATER
600G MONKFISH TAIL,
    CUT INTO 50G CHUNKS

FOR THE TRIPLE-COOKED CHIPS
1.2KG RED POTATOES, PEELED
    AND CUT INTO CHUNKY CHIPS
JUICE OF 2 LEMONS MIXED
    WITH 1 LITRE WATER
1 LITRE VEGETABLE OIL
    FOR DEEP FRYING

First make the tartare sauce. Wrap the grated cucumber tightly in a tea-towel to remove any excess moisture – this ensures the dip retains a nice, thick consistency and doesn't become overly watery. Place all the ingredients in a small bowl and mix together thoroughly. Chill for a couple of hours to allow the flavours to mature.

Next make the batter. Combine all the dry ingredients in a bowl, then remove two tablespoons and reserve (to coat the fish). Make a well in the centre of the dry ingredients. Gradually pour in the lager and water, stirring with a wooden spoon until it's lump-free. Chill for an hour to allow the batter to come together.

Meanwhile, crack on with the triple-cooked chips, (they are blanched in water, then blanched in oil at a low temperature, then deep-fried at a higher temperature). Place the potatoes in a medium pan with the water and lemon juice mixture, bring to the boil and cook for 10 minutes (they should remain al dente and not be cooked through). Drain and pat dry with kitchen paper.

Heat the oil in a large deep pan to 130°C (check with a kitchen thermometer or see page 22) and fry the chips for around 12 minutes (they shouldn't be too coloured at all at this stage). Remove with a slotted spoon and place on a plate lined with kitchen paper to soak up any excess oil.

Increase the temperature of the oil to 180°C and fry the chips again, this time for 3–4 minutes, until they are dark golden. Once cooked, remove with a slotted spoon and transfer to a baking tray in an oven preheated at 120°C/gas mark ½ to keep warm for no longer than 15 minutes.

Coat the monkfish nuggets in the reserved flour mix and then in the batter. Use one hand for flouring the fish and the other for handling the battered fish, otherwise you'll end up with clumps of flour and batter all over your fingers! Deep-fry at 180°C until golden brown (about 3–4 minutes). Remove with a slotted spoon and place on a plate lined with kitchen paper to soak up any excess oil. Serve with the hot chips and tartare sauce.

BUFFETS & CROWD PLEASERS

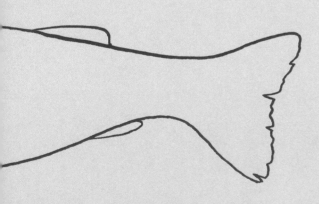

FILLET OF SEA BASS, WILTED SPINACH, LEMON & SHRIMP BUTTER & CRUSHED POTATOES

This simple, classic little number is really quick to make but impressive to serve, so listen up! Serves 4

FOR THE POTATOES
600G RATTE POTATOES
SPLASH OF GOOD-QUALITY
   OLIVE OIL
SALT AND FRESHLY GROUND
BLACK PEPPER
JUICE OF 2 LEMONS
2 TABLESPOONS FINELY CHOPPED
   FRESH SORREL, PLUS A FEW
   LEAVES TO GARNISH

FOR THE FISH
DRIZZLE OF OLIVE OIL
4 SEA BASS FILLETS

FOR THE SHRIMP BUTTER
100G BUTTER
JUICE AND ZEST OF 1 LEMON
200G ATLANTIC SHRIMPS, PEELED
2 TABLESPOONS FINELY CHOPPED
   PARSLEY

FOR THE SPINACH
KNOB OF BUTTER
SPLASH OF WHITE WINE
200G FRESH SPINACH

Place the potatoes in a large saucepan of boiling water and cook for 20 minutes. Once cooked, drain and add a splash of olive oil, salt and black pepper, the juice of 1 lemon and the sorrel, and boom! Roughly crush the potatoes using the back of a fork.

For the sea bass, heat a drizzle of oil in a frying pan over a medium heat and add the sea bass, skin-side down in the pan. Cook until crispy, for about 4 minutes, then carefully turn over and fry for a further minute. Sea bass takes no time at all to cook and needs looking after, so keep an eye out.

For the shrimp butter, place the butter in a saucepan with the lemon zest and whisk in the lemon juice over a medium heat. Add the shrimps and cook for about 1 minute, then stir in the parsley, remove from the heat and set aside.

For the spinach, heat the butter in a saucepan and add the wine. Reduce for a couple of minutes, then cook the spinach for 1 minute.

Place the spinach in the centre of each plate, cover with the crushed potatoes and rest a sea bass fillet on top. Drizzle with the shrimp butter and garnish with a couple of sorrel leaves.

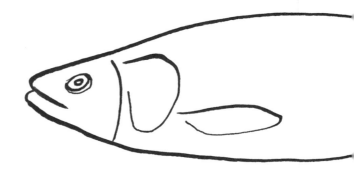

THE ULTIMATE SEAFOOD BUFFET

A great selection of fishy dishes make up this buffet – great for a summer's afternoon, maybe with a glass or two of something chilled …! Serves 6

BAKED SEA BASS

We're big seafood lovers in the Garcia household, and there aren't many better ways to bring out the best in a fish than to cook it whole, so the bones, skin and all help to develop a beautiful flavour on the flesh, whilst the inside stuffing helps to steam cook it also. Yum!

```
50G FRESH DILL, CHOPPED
50G FRESH CHIVES, SNIPPED
30G FRESH MARJORAM, LEAVES
   ONLY, CHOPPED
1 TABLESPOON DRIED OREGANO
1 GARLIC CLOVE, CRUSHED
30G FRESH BASIL, LEAVES ONLY,
   CHOPPED
1 TABLESPOON OLIVE OIL
1 WHOLE SEA BASS, APPROXIMATELY
   600G, GUTTED, SCALED AND
   SKIN SCORED
130G CHERRY TOMATOES, CHOPPED
2 LEMONS, SLICED
40ML DILL AND LEMON OIL
   (SEE OPPOSITE)
```

Preheat the oven to 180°C/gas mark 4.

Combine all the herbs with the garlic in a small bowl together with the olive oil. Stuff the cavity of the sea bass first with the herbs and then with the tomatoes and lemon. Place on a baking tray and drizzle over the Dill and Lemon Oil, bake for 25 minutes or until the fish is all opaque and beginning to fall away from the bone when pulled.

Serve on a bed of Orange, Fennel and Spinach Salad. Now you're ready to tuck in!

ORANGE, FENNEL & SPINACH SALAD

The Baked Sea Bass is served over this salad – the heat from the fish lightly wilts the spinach.

```
3 ORANGES
2 FENNEL BULBS, VERY
   FINELY SLICED
1 CELERY STICK, FINELY SLICED
150G SPINACH
```

Peel and segment the oranges, over a serving dish large enough to hold the sea bass, so that any juices drip straight into the bowl. Place the segments into the dish with the remaining ingredients. Season and combine, ready for the Baked Sea Bass to go on top.

GARLIC PRAWNS

I think it gives a much more rustic approach to the buffet to serve prawns with the shells on and I also love eating the juice from the head… the best bit in my opinion, or maybe I'm just a bit weird?

```
6 TIGER PRAWNS, SHELL ON
½ RED CHILLI, DESEEDED AND
   FINELY CHOPPED
1 BUNCH CURLED LEAF PARSLEY,
FINELY CHOPPED, PLUS EXTRA
   TO GARNISH
50ML OLIVE OIL
2 GARLIC CLOVES, CRUSHED
JUICE OF 1 LEMON
LEMON WEDGES, TO GARNISH
```

Place all the ingredients apart from the lemon juice in a mixing bowl. Cover and set aside to marinate for 1 hour in the fridge.

Heat a griddle pan over a high heat and drain the prawns. Cook them for 90 seconds on each side, until dark pink. Whilst cooking, drizzle over the lemon juice.

Garnish with fresh parsley and lemon wedges.

TUNA SALAD

This is a simple version of a tuna niçoise – colourful, fresh and, above all, really tasty.

ZEST AND JUICE OF 2 LEMONS
300G POTATOES, CUT INTO
   2CM CHUNKS
100G BABY CORN, TRIMMED
   AND BLANCHED
200G GREEN BEANS, TRIMMED
   AND BLANCHED
6 ASPARAGUS SPEARS
12 QUAILS' EGGS
2 TUNA STEAKS
½ RED ONION, THINLY SLICED
SALT AND FRESHLY GROUND
   BLACK PEPPER
DILL AND LEMON OIL, TO SERVE

Place 500ml water in a medium pan with the lemon juice and zest, the juiced lemon halves and a good pinch of salt and bring to the boil. Place the potato chunks, baby corn, green beans and asparagus spears in the water and blanch.

Remove the asparagus spears after 3 minutes, the baby corn and beans after 4-5 minutes, and the potatoes after around 15 minutes, or until just cooked. Once cooked, run under cold water and allow to cool. In our pop-ups we use a corer to cut the potato pieces into perfect cylinders, but it's not overly necessary! Regardless, all the vegetables should now have a slightly lemony flavour to them, which is exactly what we want!

Place the quails' eggs in a medium pan of boiling salted water and boil them for 1 minute 50 seconds. Drain and cool under cold running water for a couple of minutes. The cold water 'shocks' the eggs and removes the membrane from the shell... we hope! Peel and halve the eggs – they should still be slightly runny.

Lightly season the tuna steaks and place a griddle pan over a high heat, with a splash of olive oil, and cook for around 1 minute on each side. Cut into 1.5cm slices.

Place all the salad ingredients in a bowl and dress with Dill and Lemon Oil just before serving.

DILL & LEMON OIL

An aromatic dressing to drizzle over the Tuna Salad and the Baked Sea Bass.

100ML EXTRA VIRGIN OLIVE OIL
JUICE OF 2 LEMONS PLUS
   1 EXTRA LEMON (FOR A REALLY
   ZINGY TASTE!)
BUNCH OF DILL, FINELY CHOPPED

Heat the olive oil and lemon juice in a small pan over a very low heat, just so you can still dip your finger in. Whisk thoroughly until combined. Add the chopped dill whilst it's still warm, and place in an airtight jar or Kilner jar to cool and infuse for at least one day. Serve cold, and add a little more fresh lemon juice for an extra kick if required. Prepare up to four days in advance.

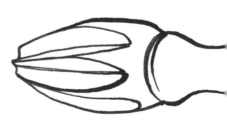

BAKED SEA BASS
ORANGE, FENNEL & SPINACH SALAD

TUNA SALAD

GARLIC PRAWNS

GRAVLAX SALMON CURED IN GIN

A SEAFOOD COCKTAIL

This is perfect for a Christmas Day starter – lots of prep, but then you're laughing! It's a combination of lots of fabulous dishes that can be made at different times in the run up to the big day. Serves 10

GRAVLAX SALMON CURED IN GIN

Super easy to make and people love it! It can be made well in advance and will keep for well over a week if wrapped in clingfilm tightly after each use.

```
1 TABLESPOON PEPPERCORNS
2 TABLESPOONS JUNIPER BERRIES
80G GRANULATED SUGAR
80G MALDON SEA SALT
6 TABLESPOONS CHOPPED
   FRESH DILL
70ML GIN
2 X 500G SALMON FILLETS
```

Place a layer of clingfilm along the top of a chopping board.

Using a pestle and mortar, lightly crush the peppercorns and juniper berries. Add the sugar, salt, dill and gin and mix.

Place one of the salmon fillets, skin side down, on the chopping board, and smother it with the contents of the bowl. Then place the second side of salmon directly on top, so flesh is on flesh, and wrap tightly in clingfilm until it's sealed. Place in a deep tray in the fridge, and place a heavy weight such as chopping board or heavy tins on top. This will draw the moisture out of the salmon and 'cure' it. The process takes two days. Drain the liquid from the tray every 12 hours, and flip it round at least once.

After two days, wipe off the curing mix with kitchen paper, skin the fillets and slice thinly to serve.

AVOCADO CREAM

This goes really well with the salmon, and is also super quick and easy to do. Prepare it up to one day in advance and keep in the fridge.

```
1 AVOCADO, PITTED AND ROUGHLY
   CHOPPED
80G CRÈME FRAÎCHE
½ LEMON
SALT AND FRESHLY GROUND
   BLACK PEPPER
```

Place the avocado and crème fraîche in a small bowl with a squeeze of lemon juice. Season and blend together until nice and smooth ... voilà!

CONFIT SALMON IN MAPLE SYRUP

For me the sweet oakiness of the maple syrup works really well with salmon. You've heard of honey-glazed salmon ... well, move over ,there's a maple in town!

```
10 X 30G SQUARES SALMON
   FILLET
250ML OLIVE OIL
250ML MAPLE SYRUP
```

Place the syrup and oil in a small pan, and heat to 75°C (check with a kitchen thermometer). Be careful not to overheat or the salmon will be overcooked. Drop in the salmon pieces ensuring they are fully submerged, and cover with foil before taking off the heat. Check after 30 minutes, they will be perfect. Once cooked, remove the salmon pieces with a fish slice and drain on some kitchen paper. You can prepare this upto 1 day in advance and serve it cold.

BEETROOT THREE WAYS

As a kid I wasn't a fan of beetroot, and then from the age of about 13, I remember giving it a go again after coming home from school … it tasted incredible! Earthy and full of flavour. So I raided all things beetroot from the fridge that night. Next day, I went to the bathroom, only to run to my parents, almost in tears, as I thought I was seriously ill … Loving beetroot can have, shall we say, 'colourful' side effects!

CURED

1 RAW BEETROOT, PEELED AND
  SLICED WAFER THIN, PREFERABLY
  USING A MANDOLIN
EXTRA VIRGIN OLIVE OIL,
  TO DRIZZLE
½ LEMON
MALDON SEA SALT

Lay the beetroot slices out on a tray. Pour over a drizzle of olive oil, a small squeeze of lemon juice, and a sprinkle of sea salt. Cover with clingfilm for 1 hour. The salt, lemon and oil should cook the beetroot to al dente.

Prepare up to 4 days in advance and keep in the fridge.

ROASTED

1 RAW BEETROOT
SALT AND FRESHLY GROUND
  BLACK PEPPER

Preheat the oven to 150°C/gas mark 2.

Season the beetroot and wrap it in foil. Roast in the oven for about 1 hour, or until cooked (pierce with a knife and if it's soft, it's ready!). Peel the skin off whilst it's still warm (it's much easier then), and cut into 1cm cubes.

Prepare up to 4 days in advance and keep in the fridge.

PICKLED

I use baby beetroot for this, it's a little more expensive, but much prettier on the plate.

10 BABY BEETROOT
100G WHITE WINE VINEGAR
35G ALL SPICE
35G WHOLE PEPPERCORNS
1 BAY LEAF
1 TEASPOON FENNEL SEEDS

Place the beetroot in a small pan of boiling water, and cook for about 45 minutes, until almost cooked, but still quite firm.

Meanwhile, place the remaining ingredients in a small pan and boil for 10 minutes to allow the flavours to all infuse. Add the boiled beetroot to the vinegar mix, and place in an airtight lidded container or Kilner jar for at least 24 hours. And voilà!

Prepare up to 2 weeks in advance and keep in the fridge in a sealed jar.

Before serving, drain on some kitchen paper, to stop the beetroot from bleeding.

MOROCCAN FEAST

Slow-braised Lamb with Salsa Verde, Moroccan-spiced Couscous and Tomato Salad plus Flatbread and Dips – this was the main course at the very first wedding I catered, and still remains a firm favourite. There are lots of lovely side dishes for everyone to tuck into and enjoy family-style – the perfect kind of food for a fun celebration. We also used to serve this as our main course on 'Slow Down Sundays', a pop-up serving only slow-roast meats. There are lots of elements to this showpiece, so without further ado, let's get cracking! Serves 8

SLOW-BRAISED LAMB

I like to treat the lamb gently and let it slowly marinate overnight and then cook it for 12½ hours – if you don't have time for this, no worries, I've suggested an alternative, not-so-slow method for cooking, too.

FOR THE MARINADE

1 TABLESPOON GROUND CUMIN
2 GARLIC CLOVES, CRUSHED
1 TABLESPOON SMOKED PAPRIKA
1 TABLESPOON CURRY POWDER
½ TABLESPOON TUMERIC
1 TABLESPOON CORIANDER
   SEEDS, CRUSHED
1 TEASPOON TAHINI PASTE
1 TEASPOON DRIED CHILLI FLAKES
2 TABLESPOONS DRIED OREGANO
100ML OLIVE OIL
SALT AND FRESHLY GROUND
   BLACK PEPPER

FOR THE LAMB

1 BONE-IN SHOULDER OF LAMB
   APPROXIMATELY 2.5KG
4 ONIONS, UNPEELED, HALVED
2 RED PEPPERS, CUT INTO CHUNKS
2 GARLIC CLOVES, CRUSHED
6 SPRIGS OF THYME, LEAVES ONLY
3 SPRIGS OF ROSEMARY,
   LEAVES ONLY

Place all the marinade ingredients in a medium bowl and stir well to create a paste. Rub the paste all over the meat then wrap it tightly in clingfilm. Set aside to marinate in the fridge, for at least 4 hours or ideally overnight to allow the flavours to work their way into the meat.

When you are ready to cook the lamb, preheat the oven to 130°C/gas mark 1, for very long cooking or to 160°C/gas mark 3 for not quite so long. Place the onions and pepper chunks in the bottom of a lidded roasting tray. Unwrap the lamb and place it on the veg. Lightly score the top of the joint, and sit the garlic, thyme and rosemary leaves in the score lines. Pour 700ml water into the tray, cover the lamb with baking parchment, then place the lid, or some foil, on the roasting tray.

The lamb is best cooked low and slow! In a perfect world, I would cook this overnight, for around 12 hours at the lower temperature, and then remove the lid and increase the heat to 200°C/gas mark 6, to crisp up the top for around 30 minutes. Alternatively, you could cook it at the medium temperature for 3½ hours, and a further 30 minutes at 200°C/gas mark 6. That should do the trick also, but the slower it cooks, the more time the flavours have to develop within the meat, and create the desired 'melt in the mouth' texture.

To serve up this delight, take the whole joint to the table, show off your hard work, and then simply pull it apart with two forks. The meat should shred so easily that even the worst knife handler wouldn't have a problem!

SALSA VERDE

Salsa verde is usually very popular with fish dishes, but I'm a huge fan of it with lamb, and as an accompaniment to this dish in particular. Herby and sharp, it packs a real punch which contrasts well with the rich lamb.

5 TABLESPOONS ROUGHLY CHOPPED
   FRESH FLAT-LEAF PARSLEY
2 TABLESPOONS ROUGHLY CHOPPED
   FRESH MINT LEAVES
1 TABLESPOON ROUGHLY CHOPPED
   FRESH DILL
3 TABLESPOONS CAPERS, DRAINED
6 ANCHOVY FILLETS, DRAINED
1 GARLIC CLOVE
1 TEASPOON DIJON MUSTARD
JUICE OF 1 LEMON
150ML EXTRA VIRGIN OLIVE OIL

Place all the ingredients in a food processor, and whiz to the consistency you prefer. Some people like to keep it rustic and chunky, so feel free to do so, but I prefer it to be almost like an oily paste. Serve on the side, or generously drizzle over the lamb!

MOROCCAN-SPICED COUSCOUS

This can be prepped in advance and served cold, so get this one out the way whilst the lamb is doing it's thing!

3 TABLESPOONS OLIVE OIL, PLUS
   EXTRA FOR COOKING THE VEG
150G RED PEPPER, DESEEDED AND
   CUT INTO 1CM CHUNKS
150G COURGETTE, CUT INTO
   1CM SLICES
500G COUSCOUS
1 TABLESPOON CURRY POWDER
1 TABLESPOON GROUND NUTMEG
1 TABLESPOON GROUND CUMIN
1 TEASPOON GROUND CINNAMON
1 TABLESPOON GROUND GINGER
1 TABLESPOON GROUND TURMERIC
2 GARLIC CLOVES, CRUSHED
ZEST AND JUICE OF 1 ORANGE
1 LITRE HOT VEGETABLE STOCK
BUNCH OF CORIANDER
BUNCH OF MINT
400G CAN CHICKPEAS
50G RAISINS
3 FRESH APRICOTS, STONED AND
   CUT INTO 1CM PIECES
100G TOASTED FLAKED ALMONDS
SALT AND FRESHLY GROUND
   BLACK PEPPER

Place a griddle pan on a high heat. Lightly rub with olive oil. Season the peppers and courgettes, and cook for around 2 minutes on each side, until char lines appear and they are cooked through. Set to one side.

Place the couscous in a heatproof mixing bowl and combine with the dried spices, garlic and orange zest. Pour over enough hot stock to just cover the couscous. Cover the bowl with a tea towel and leave for 5 minutes.

Give the couscous a good mix with your hands, to create the desired 'fluffy' effect, running the grains through your index finger and thumb. Add the remaining ingredients to the bowl, stir well and Bob's your uncle!

FLATBREADS

These are so quick and easy to make. They are widely regarded as the earliest form of bread, so consider this a history lesson!

250G PLAIN FLOUR, PLUS EXTRA
   FOR DUSTING
1 TEASPOON GROUND CUMIN
1 TEASPOON CURRY POWDER
1 TEASPOON GROUND CORIANDER
SALT AND FRESHLY GROUND
   BLACK PEPPER

Place all the ingredients in a mixing bowl and stir to combine. Slowly add approximately 100ml cold water and stir until a firm dough is formed.

Divide the dough into 8 equal balls, and roll out on a worksurface dusted with flour, using a rolling pin, to a thickness of about 3mm. The dough should have a little bit of elasticity to it.

Place a non-stick frying pan on the hob on a high heat. Cook the flatbreads for around 1 minute on each side, or until scorch marks begin to appear on both sides.

These can be reheated in the oven for just a couple of minutes at 150°C before serving to give a lovely warm flatbread.

TSATZIKI

This versatile dish goes so well with lamb, see page 15 for the recipe.

BABA GHANOUSH

This is one of my favourite dips ever. So simple, but so rewarding in terms of smoky flavour. To me, an aubergine is at its best after it's been smoked.

2 AUBERGINES
JUICE OF 1 LEMON
1 TEASPOON CUMIN
½ TEASPOON SMOKED PAPRIKA
1 GARLIC CLOVE, FINELY CHOPPED
SALT AND FRESHLY GROUND
   BLACK PEPPER

Preheat the oven to 180°C/gas mark 4.

To create the smoky flavour, we need to char the aubergines. This can be done either on a barbecue, over an open fire, or using a pair of tongs, and rotating the whole aubergine over the flame on a gas hob, to 'burn' the skin. Alternatively, you could char them under a hot grill for about 10 minutes on each side, but for best results, you want a naked flame. Once charred on all sides, place on a baking tray and bake for 20 minutes.

Peel off the charred skin and transfer the flesh to a mixing bowl. Add the remaining ingredients and blend to a smooth consistency. Season to taste, done!

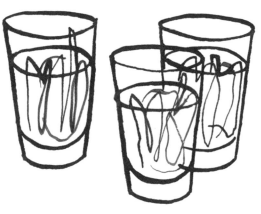

HUMMUS

This is such a favourite these days. You can't go anywhere without seeing a pot of hummus. Whether it's in the supermarket, at work or even on the train! Popular as an accompaniment to the lamb, or also just with some crudités here's a DIY hummus!

400G CAN CHICKPEAS, DRAINED
JUICE OF 1 LEMON
3 GARLIC CLOVES
2 TABLESPOONS OLIVE OIL
1 TEASPOON GROUND CUMIN
PAPRIKA, TO GARNISH

Place all the ingredients in the food processor with 2 tablespoons of water, and let it do its thing for 3-4 minutes until everything is super smooth. Add a little more water if you'd prefer it a little looser. Garnish with a dusting of paprika.

TOMATO, FETA & RED ONION SALAD

A lovely, juicy summer salad that works perfectly as part of this buffet, so just chuck all these ingredients into a bowl with a cheeky white balsamic dressing and you're away! Heritage tomatoes are also widely known as heirloom tomatoes.

600G HERITAGE TOMATOES,
  CUT INTO VARIOUS DIFFERENT
  SHAPES AND SIZES
180G FETA CHEESE, CUT
  INTO CHUNKS
1 RED ONION, HALVED AND
  FINELY SLICED
2 CELERY STICKS, CHOPPED
  INTO SMALL PIECES

FOR THE DRESSING
2 TABLESPOONS WHITE
  BALSAMIC VINEGAR
5 TABLESPOONS EXTRA
  VIRGIN OLIVE OIL
PINCH OF SALT

Place the tomatoes, feta, onion and celery in a serving dish. Combine the dressing ingredients, mixing well, then drizzle all over the salad.

The Moroccan feast is ready to enjoy!

PULLED PORK CRUMBLE WITH APPLE PURÉE & CAJUN SLAW

Now, everybody loves a bit of pulled pork! It goes down a storm at weddings when everyone needs to soak up the free booze they've consumed, and also in a bun with a lovely slaw. Nothing wrong with that, but we're doing a little twist by combining a few bits to do something a little bit different! If you want to serve this in a mini casserole dish, feel free, but I think it looks great, and more modern, as an open crumble. Serves 4

1 QUANTITY OF PULLED PORK
   (PAGE 65) (REDUCE THE
   COOKING LIQUOR FROM
   THE PORK UNTIL YOU GET A
   DELICIOUS, THICK SAUCE)

FOR THE CRUMBLE
100G PLAIN FLOUR
30G BUTTER
20G PUMPKIN SEEDS
20G FLAKED ALMONDS
30G OATS
30G SUNFLOWER SEEDS

FOR THE APPLE PURÉE
2 APPLES, PEELED AND CUT
   INTO CHUNKS
500ML APPLE JUICE

CAJUN SLAW (PAGE 65),
   TO SERVE

Preheat the oven to 200°C/gas mark 6. Line a baking tray with baking parchment.

Place all the crumble ingredients in a bowl, then rub in the butter with your index finger and thumb until you have a coarse mix. Place on the lined tray and bake for about 15 minutes or until golden, then remove and allow to cool.

Place the apples and juice in a small pan and simmer until soft. Using a slotted spoon, transfer the apples to a blender and blitz, slowly adding the juice until you have the consistency you require. I like mine thin enough to be able to use it to give a good swipe!

To serve, swipe the apple purée across individual plates, place the slaw along the line of purée, then add a nice big dollop of the warm pulled pork (reheat in the oven once pulled with a small splash of water), and sprinkle the savoury crumble around the plate, along with a few drops of the reduced pork cooking liquor.

WILD MUSHROOM & TRUFFLE MAC & CHEESE WITH POACHED DUCK EGGS

Mac and cheese has become incredibly popular of late, and what's not to love? It's incredibly easy to do it well. I have a chap who forages my mushrooms. Rather a strange fellow who looks like he may have swallowed a couple of the dodgy kind in his time, but all he ever picks me are truly amazing wild varieties! I try to use a smoky Wensleydale for this dish, but feel free to mix up the cheeses as you wish. The poached duck eggs add a real richness, creating something quite special. Serves 4

400G MACARONI
15ML TRUFFLE OIL
1½ ONIONS, SLICED
2 GARLIC CLOVES, FINELY
    CHOPPED
200G WILD MUSHROOMS, OR ANY
    VARIETY YOU PREFER (OYSTER
    MUSHROOMS WORK WELL)
150G COARSE, WHITE
    BREADCRUMBS
1 TABLESPOON WHITE WINE
    VINEGAR
4 DUCK EGGS
SALT

FOR THE CHEESE SAUCE
50G BUTTER
50G PLAIN FLOUR
100ML WHITE WINE
200ML SEMI-SKIMMED MILK
150G SMOKED WENSLEYDALE,
    GRATED
150G STRONG CHEDDAR, GRATED
150G BRIE, FINELY CHOPPED
1 TABLESPOON DRIED OREGANO
SALT AND FRESHLY GROUND
    BLACK PEPPER
TRUFFLE SHAVINGS, TO GARNISH
    (IF YOU'RE FEELING FLUSH!)

Preheat the oven to 200°C/gas mark 6.

Bring a pan of salted water up to the boil, and cook the macaroni according to the packet instructions (11 minutes, usually). Drain and set aside.

Meanwhile, heat the truffle oil in a medium frying pan and fry the onions and garlic until softened, then add the wild mushrooms and continue to cook for a further 3 minutes before setting to one side.

To make the cheese sauce, place the butter in a large saucepan and add the flour, stirring continuously until the butter is completely melted. Slowly add the wine and then the milk, whisking vigorously to prevent any lumps forming. The sauce should coat the back of the spoon, but not be too gloopy. Add two-thirds of the cheeses, along with the oregano, and allow them to melt into the sauce. Season with a pinch of salt and pepper.

Once the sauce is done, add the mushroom mixture and pasta, and give everything a good mix before transferring to a 15cm ovenproof dish. Scatter the remaining cheese and the breadcrumbs over, then bake for 12 minutes, or until the top is golden brown.

Meanwhile, bring a medium pan of water to the boil, then reduce to a simmer. Add the white wine vinegar, give it a stir with a whisk, and crack in the duck eggs, and poach for 3½ minutes (they take slightly longer than hen's eggs).

Take the mac out the oven, and top with the duck eggs and some truffle shavings and boom! Ready to eat. Easy, tasty and quick!

WINTER SLAW

A delicious, crunchy and healthy winter salad. It's really cheap to make and is great as a sandwich filler or as an accompaniment to a main dish. It goes particularly well with Pulled Pork (page 65). And if you're short on time you could cheat and dollop in some ready-made mayo! Serves 6

FOR THE MAYO
2 MEDIUM EGG YOLKS
2 TABLESPOONS DIJON MUSTARD
1 TABLESPOON WHITE WINE
  VINEGAR
250ML OLIVE OIL
JUICE OF 1 LEMON

For the mayo, place the egg yolks, Dijon mustard and vinegar in a food processor and slowly add the olive oil until combined. Process until thick and pale. Season with salt and pepper, then add the lemon juice and combine. Voilà!

FOR THE SALAD
150G RED CABBAGE, THINLY
  SLICED
½ RED ONION, THINLY SLICED
2 CARROTS, GRATED
1 APPLE, PEELED AND GRATED
100G CELERIAC, GRATED
1 CELERY STICK, FINELY
  CHOPPED
BUNCH OF FLAT-LEAF PARSLEY,
  FINELY CHOPPED
50G TOASTED FLAKED ALMONDS,
  TO GARNISH

For the salad, combine all the ingredients, except the almonds, in a serving bowl and mix in the mayo. Garnish with the toasted almonds.

CHICKEN & CHORIZO STEW WITH CRUSHED NEW POTATOES

I cooked this for the lovely Eamonn and Ruth during my first appearance on *This Morning*. If you're wanting to serve a crowd, simply double up on ingredients. Serves 4

FOR THE STEW
20ML OLIVE OIL
4 CHICKEN THIGHS, SKIN ON
3 GARLIC CLOVES, CRUSHED
2 RED ONIONS, THINLY SLICED
1 CELERY STICK, FINELY DICED
100G CHORIZO, CUT INTO
   1CM CUBES
1 COURGETTE, ROUGHLY CHOPPED
   INTO 1CM THICK SLICES
2 RED PEPPERS, DESEEDED
   AND ROUGHLY CHOPPED INTO
   2CM PIECES
175ML WHITE WINE
250ML PASSATA
400G CAN CHOPPED TOMATOES
2 SPRIGS OF THYME

FOR THE POTATOES
800G NEW POTATOES, WASHED
   AND HALVED
BUNCH OF FLAT-LEAF PARSLEY,
   FINELY CHOPPED
JUICE OF 1 LEMON
SALT AND FRESHLY GROUND
   BLACK PEPPER

Preheat the oven to 150°C/gas mark 2.

In a heavy saucepan, heat the olive oil and fry the chicken thighs skin-side down until golden brown, then place in a medium roasting tin.

Add the garlic, onions and celery to the pan and fry until softened. Add the chorizo, courgette, peppers, wine, passata, tomatoes and thyme, and simmer for 10 minutes.

Pour the sauce over the chicken. Bake for 40 minutes, covered with foil, and then for a further 10 minutes, uncovered.

Meanwhile, cook the potatoes in a medium pan of boiling salted water for 15–20 minutes, or until soft. Lightly mash the potatoes, leaving the skins on. Stir in the parsley, lemon juice and seasoning. And bosh! Ready to serve with the stew.

RESTAURANT-STANDARD DAUPHINOISE POTATOES

Have you ever wondered how in a restaurant the Dauphinoise are
all in neat squares or circles, yet at home, they're usually spooned
all over the place in a creamy potatoey pile? Maybe you haven't!
But I'm going to show you how. If you're feeling a little adventurous,
why not layer your potatoes with all sorts of interesting bits?
Confit duck perhaps? Or wild mushrooms, or a cheeky bit of foie gras?
Get experimenting! Serves 4

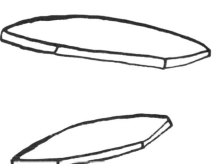

500ML DOUBLE CREAM
2 GARLIC CLOVES, FINELY
   CHOPPED
2 SPRIGS OF FRESH THYME
1 BAY LEAF
PINCH OF NUTMEG
800G WAXY, CHARLOTTE POTATOES
2 TABLESPOONS DRIED HERBES
   DE PROVENCE
1 TABLESPOON DRIED GARLIC
SALT AND FRESHLY GROUND
   BLACK PEPPER

Preheat the oven to 150°C/gas mark 2. Line a small
roasting dish with greaseproof paper.

Place the cream in a small pan with the garlic,
thyme, bay leaf and nutmeg, and allow to
infuse on a low heat.

Meanwhile, slice the potatoes as thinly as possible
using a mandolin, food processor or by hand.

Layer the potatoes in the dish, and in between each
layer, sprinkle some salt, pepper, dried herbs and
dried garlic, followed by a drizzle of the infused
cream. Continue until all the potatoes are used up.
Press down the potatoes and bake for about 1 hour
20 minutes, or until golden on top and cooked all
the way through.

Remove from the oven and place a baking tray on
top of the potatoes, top with a heavy weight and
allow to cool for a few hours. This will help make
the Dauphinoise look restaurant-style when it comes
to serving, by pressing the potato slices together.
The starch in the potatoes helps to act as a glue!
Once cooled, you can cut the Dauphinoise into
squares or circles, and reheat in the oven.

To reheat, place on a baking tray in the oven for about
20 minutes, or until hot all the way through. These
could also be served straight from the oven if you want
a lovely tray of 'dauphies' ... but for that restaurant-style
finish, you'll need to press them.

FOOLPROOF ROOT VEGETABLES

To me, roast root veg are a staple for many a winter dish, and can help make or break a roast dinner. The root veg family are a tasty old bunch. I like to blanch all of my veg first, to ensure you don't get that woody flavour that can sometimes occur. Serves 6 (as a side dish)

600G CARROTS, HALVED
    LENGTHWAYS
600G PARSNIPS, HALVED
    LENGTHWAYS
800G TURNIPS, QUARTERED
2 CELERY STICKS, CUT
    INTO CHUNKS
3 TABLESPOONS CLEAR HONEY
    (SPANISH BLOSSOM IF
    POSSIBLE)
2 TABLESPOONS TRUFFLE OIL
SPRIG OF THYME, LEAVES ONLY
SPRIG OF ROSEMARY,
    LEAVES ONLY
2 GARLIC CLOVES, CRUSHED
100G BUTTER, CUT INTO
    10G CUBES
SALT AND FRESHLY GROUND
    BLACK PEPPER

Preheat the oven to 200°C/gas mark 6.

Bring a large pan of salted water to the boil. Add the carrots, parsnips and turnips and blanch them for 7 minutes. Drain and allow to cool.

Place the blanched veg and celery on a roasting tray with the remaining ingredients, dotting the cubes of butter around the veg. Season well and roast for 20 minutes or until the veg starts to caramelise slightly – and there you have it!

JIM'S TUNA NICOISE

This is a lovely summer dish, it looks and tastes impressive, and is relatively good for the waistline! It's a combination of lots of delicious different elements – seared tuna steak, lemon-boiled potatoes, griddled asparagus, baby corn, demi-boiled quails' eggs, *sauce vierge*, pickled cucumber and wild garlic purée, but it is really worth the effort! Serves 4

330ML OLIVE OIL
JUICE AND ZEST OF 3 LEMONS
1 TOMATO, FLESH ONLY,
   FINELY DICED
½ RED PEPPER, FINELY DICED
½ COURGETTE, FINELY DICED
1 SHALLOT, FINELY DICED
BUNCH OF FLAT-LEAF PARSLEY,
   CHOPPED
6 QUAILS' EGGS
1KG POTATOES, CUT INTO
   CYLINDERS USING A CORER
8 BABY CORN
200G WILD GARLIC LEAVES
½ CUCUMBER, CUT INTO RIBBONS
   WITH A RIBBON PEELER AND
   THEN CUT INTO THIN
   STRING-LIKE STRIPS
3 TABLESPOONS WHITE
   BALSAMIC VINEGAR
8 ASPARAGUS SPEARS
4 TUNA STEAKS, APPROXIMATELY
   150G EACH AND ABOUT
   2CM THICK
SALT AND FRESHLY GROUND
   BLACK PEPPER

First up, let's get the *sauce vierge* boshed out. This goes well with so much seafood and is basically olive oil with vegetables, herbs and lemon juice. It's subtlety allows the fish to beam! Heat 200ml of the olive oil in a small pan, to around 80°C (check with a kitchen thermometer) and whisk in the juice of 1 lemon, then take off the heat. Stir in the diced veg and chopped parsley and allow to cool.

Hard boil the quails' eggs ahead of time, then peel and cut into halves to serve.

Bring 1 litre of water to the boil in a medium pan with the juice of 2 lemons and the squeezed-out lemon shells. Cook the potatoes for 3 minutes and then add the baby corn to the pan and cook for a further 7 minutes. Drain and set aside.

For the wild garlic purée, bring a small pan of water to the boil and blanch the leaves for around 20 seconds. Drain and transfer to a food processor, season and slowly add 120ml of olive oil until a smooth consistency is reached. Transfer to a jug or a squeezy bottle if you have one.

Next, place the cucumber strings, vinegar and 3 tablespoons water in a bowl for about 20 minutes. Drain before serving.

Place a griddle pan on the hob over a high heat. Season the asparagus and tuna steak well and with the remaining oil, lightly grease the griddle pan. Fry the asparagus spears for around 3 minutes or until they are charred but still have a little crunch.

Reheat the potatoes and baby corn in a pan of boiling water for 1 minute.

Pan-fry the tuna steak on the griddle for 90 seconds on each side – I think it's best served still very pink on the inside. If you prefer, cook the tuna steak on a preheated barbie for around 2 minutes on each side and it will be deelish! Cut diagonally into slices.

To serve, dot the veg around the plate, leaning it up against each other, and place a spoonful of the cucumber in the middle. Sit the tuna steak on top, dot the garlic purée around and drizzle over the *sauce vierge*.

RUSSIAN SALAD

Having cooked for many a Russian, both in Courchevel and London, I'd like to think I've earned my stripes when it comes to throwing together a Russian Salad, also known as an Olivier Salad, as it was invented in the 1800s by a Russian chef called Lucien Olivier. Serves 6

8 SLICES SERRANO HAM
800G BABY NEW POTATOES,
    HALVED
150G CARROTS, FINELY DICED
150G PEAS, FRESH OR FROZEN
4 DUCK EGGS
3 TABLESPOONS CHOPPED
    GHERKINS
1 TABLESPOON CAPERS IN BRINE,
    RINSED AND DRAINED
SMALL BUNCH OF DILL, CHOPPED
1 QUANTITY OF MAYONNAISE
    (SEE PAGE 51)
SALT AND FRESHLY GROUND
    BLACK PEPPER
SMALL BUNCH OF DILL, FINELY
    CHOPPED, TO GARNISH

Preheat the oven to 200°C/gas mark 6.

Place the slices of Serrano ham (grouse was originally used!) on a roasting tray, and bake for 20 minutes, or until really crispy. Break the ham into shards and set aside.

Meanwhile, bring a medium pan of salted water to the boil, add the potatoes and cook for around 15 minutes, or until tender. Drain, and allow to cool.

Bring a second medium pan of salted water to the boil and add the carrots. Cook for around 4 minutes before adding the peas and cooking for another 4. You still want to have some crunch in the carrots and some colour in your peas! Drain all the veg.

Cook the duck eggs in another pan of boiling water for 8 minutes before removing, and running under the cold tap. Once cooled completely, peel them and chop them into quarters.

Combine all the ingredients in a serving bowl, stirring well to coat everything with mayonnaise. Finish with a pinch of salt and pepper and a sprinkle of fresh dill – easy peasy!

BBQ & BURGERS

DUCK BURGERS WITH ORANGE & EARL GREY RELISH

Now this really is a quacking good burger... I've used more puns for this burger than I care to remember, so I'll save you the pain. Suffice to say, it's slicker than your average burger! I have held countless Burger and Bordeaux evenings in London, where we offer a duck or a lobster burger alongside half a bottle of white or red Bordeaux. Both burgers are a fantastic alternative to the normal beef burger, and are just as easy to make, but for me the duck is the winner here. We serve this delight topped with beetroot, Gruyère and oyster mushrooms and a delicious, sweet chutney which works really well with the meatiness of the burger and the earthiness of the beetroot and mushrooms. Serves 4

FOR THE CHUTNEY (THE REAL STAR OF THE SHOW)
6 SHALLOTS, FINELY SLICED
20ML VEGETABLE OIL
KNOB OF BUTTER
1 LITRE ORANGE JUICE
4 TABLESPOONS CLEAR HONEY
2 TABLESPOONS EARL GREY TEA LEAVES OR 2 EARL GREY TEABAGS, RIPPED OPEN
2 TABLESPOONS DEMERARA SUGAR

FOR THE BURGERS
KNOB OF BUTTER
4 SHALLOTS, DICED
1 GARLIC CLOVE, FINELY CHOPPED
2 TABLESPOONS CHINESE FIVE SPICE POWDER
50G COARSE, DRIED BREADCRUMBS
600G DUCK BREAST, SKIN ON, MINCED (IF YOU ASK YOUR BUTCHER NICELY, THEY SHOULD BE HAPPY TO DO THIS FOR YOU)
SALT AND FRESHLY GROUND BLACK PEPPER

FOR THE TOPPINGS
150G OYSTER MUSHROOMS, SLICED
GRATED GRUYÈRE CHEESE
4 THIN SLICES OF COOKED BEETROOT
4 BRIOCHE BUNS, TO SERVE

First thing we need to do is get the chutney on the hob and reducing, so put the shallots in a medium pan, together with the oil and butter. Once the shallots are softened, add all the remaining ingredients and reduce on a medium heat for around 1¾ hours, or until brown and thick. You'll need to stir the mixture occasionally to prevent the shallots from burning on the bottom of the pan. Remember, too, that once cooled the chutney will set even more, so try not to reduce it too much – just until it heavily coats the back of the spoon.

Whilst the chutney is bubbling away, get on to the burgers. Heat the butter in a medium frying pan and fry the shallots and garlic for 4–5 minutes until softened. Add the five spice powder and seasoning, then turn off the heat and allow to cool.

Once cooled, transfer the cooked shallots to a mixing bowl, add the breadcrumbs and minced duck, and get your hands in there to mix thoroughly. Divide into four equal patties and shape using your hands, or use a ring mould if you have one. Place on a tray, cover and put in the fridge to set for 30 minutes, so they hold their shape when fried.

Preheat the oven to 200°C/gas mark 6. Line a baking tray with baking parchment.

Heat a frying pan until hot, then seal the burgers over a high heat for around 2 minutes on each side, until well coloured, then transfer to the lined tray and bake for 8 minutes for lovely medium-rare duck burgers.

Whilst the patties are in the oven, use the same pan to sauté the oyster mushrooms in the lovely duck fat left in the pan. I'd advise (but your doctor probably wouldn't) mopping the pan with the brioche bun before serving for a true duck burger finish.

Serve the burgers in the split buns, topped with the cheese, beetroot and mushrooms, with a generous blob of chutney on the side. Enjoy!

BUILD YOUR OWN ULTIMATE BURGER!

Every summer we get inundated with requests to do barbecues. And inevitably, people ask for a range of different extras to have on their burgers. So, we decided to create a really fun buffet-style station offering every topping imaginable. Guests move along the line, picking and choosing as they go... the majority will be modest, but there's always a few where you're not sure if the diner is going to try to eat it or climb it! Nevertheless, it's a great idea if you're organising an informal summer party. Serves 4

FOR THE BURGERS

1 TABLESPOON OLIVE OIL
2 SHALLOTS, FINELY DICED
1 GARLIC CLOVE, FINELY CHOPPED
600G GOOD-QUALITY MINCED BEEF
  (MINCED RUMP IS MY
  FAVOURITE, PARTICULARLY
  ABERDEEN ANGUS, BUT
  WHICHEVER YOU PREFER)
50G BREADCRUMBS
SMALL BUNCH OF PARSLEY
1 TABLESPOON DRIED OREGANO
1 EGG YOLK
SALT AND FRESHLY GROUND
  BLACK PEPPER

So let's start with the burgers! Place the olive oil in a frying pan over a medium heat. Add the shallots and garlic and fry for 4 minutes until softened, but not golden. Once cooked, allow to cool.

Place the remaining ingredients in a large mixing bowl, and combine thoroughly with your hands... get stuck in! Separate the contents of the bowl into four equal-sized balls, and shape into patties before transferring to the fridge to set. This will help to stop the burger from falling apart when you cook it.

Light the barbecue, and allow the flames to die down if it's a charcoal one, before cooking your burgers. Press them down onto the rack, and turn a few times during cooking. The burgers should feel firm, with a small bit of 'bounce' when squeezed for a beautiful medium burger... it depends on how hot the heat is, but a 2.5cm burger should take around 4 minutes on each side. Allow to rest for 10 minutes, covered with foil, if you can block out the smells and hunger... as I often can't!

REGULAR TOPPINGS...

SO, THE OBVIOUS EASY ONES TO OFFER ARE:

Sliced heritage tomatoes
Truffle-cured beetroot (see page 76)
Sliced raw red onions or fried onions
Fried mushrooms
Rocket or other salad leaves
Cheese – most people love a great cheese burger! It's always good to give a variety if you're feeling flush, as this helps set your burger apart:
Cheddar slices
Blue cheese, sliced
Brie, chopped
Cured meat – people tend to be quite keen on a cheeky few chorizo slices (me included, with a Spanish dad), so if a taste of the Med tickles your fancy, get it on a plate!

AND MY SPECIALITY TOPPINGS...

Treat yourself to one (or more!) of these for an extra-special, mouthwatering burger. All recipes make enough to top 4 burgers. Any extra pulled pork or chilli con carne can be added to rice or slaw for a meal in itself ... or stock up the freezer meals for those lazy days!

PULLED PORK

WE CALL PULLED PORK ON TOP OF A
BEEF PATTY PIGGY VS HERD... OH MY,
IT'S GOOD!

200G DEMERARA SUGAR
2 TABLESPOONS GROUND CUMIN
2 TABLESPOONS PAPRIKA
2 TABLESPOONS BLACK TREACLE
1 TEASPOON WORCESTERSHIRE SAUCE
1 TABLESPOON ENGLISH MUSTARD
800G BONELESS PORK SHOULDER
2 ONIONS, SLICED
2 GARLIC CLOVES, CHOPPED
1 APPLE, CUT INTO CHUNKS
1 CELERY STICK
400G CAN TOMATOES
BUNCH OF THYME
1 BAY LEAF
50ML BALSAMIC VINEGAR
SALT AND FRESHLY GROUND
   BLACK PEPPER

Mix together the sugar, cumin, paprika,
treacle, Worcestershire sauce, mustard
and seasoning. Rub over the meat, cover
then marinate for 1 hour in the fridge.

Preheat the oven to 150°C/gas mark 2.

Place the remaining ingredients in a
roasting tin with 200ml water and stir to
combine. Add the marinated pork, cover in
baking parchment, and then foil, this allows
the meat to almost steam cook. Place in the
oven and cook for 5 hours, or until tender
and falling apart.

Once cooked, remove the pork and set
aside. Transfer the cooking liquor to a
medium pan, stir well, bring to the boil
and reduce until it thickens. Season to
taste, then return the pork to the sauce.
There you have it – deliciously, saucy,
gooey, pulled pork – perfect for a burger
topping.

MAPLE BACON

8 SLICES STREAKY, SMOKED BACON
100ML MAPLE SYRUP

Soak the bacon in maple syrup, overnight if
possible. Crisp on the BBQ until golden.

CHILLI CON CARNE

FOR THOSE WHO FANCY HEADING DOWN
THE MEXICAN ROUTE.

2 TABLESPOONS VEGETABLE OIL
2 ONIONS, DICED
2 GARLIC CLOVES, FINELY CHOPPED
½ BIRD'S EYE CHILLI, DESEEDED
   AND FINELY CHOPPED
1 RED PEPPER, DESEEDED
   AND DICED
2 TABLESPOONS CAJUN SEASONING
1 TABLESPOON DRIED MARJORAM
1 TABLESPOON GROUND CUMIN
1 TABLESPOON PAPRIKA
500G MINCED BEEF
150ML RED WINE
300ML PASSATA
1 TEASPOON TOMATO PURÉE
400G CAN CHOPPED TOMATOES
400G CAN KIDNEY BEANS, DRAINED

Heat the oil in a deep frying pan over a
medium heat and fry the onions and garlic
until softened. Add the chilli, red pepper
and all the herbs and spices.

Increase the heat and add the beef. Once
it's taken on some colour, add the wine and
give it a stir, scraping up the caramelised
juices from the bottom of the pan. Add the
passata, tomato purée and tomatoes, and
bring to a simmer, then reduce to a low
heat. Add the kidney beans and bubble
away for at least 1 hour, until the sauce has
a lovely consistency and rich flavour.

CAJUN SLAW

THIS IS GREAT SERVED ON TOP
OF, OR ALONGSIDE, YOUR BURGER
AS A SIDE.

200G CARROTS, GRATED
½ RED ONION, FINELY SLICED
1 EATING APPLE (I LIKE
   BRAEBURN), CORED, PEELED
   AND GRATED
¼ RED CABBAGE, GRATED
2 TABLESPOONS CAJUN SEASONING
2 TABLESPOONS MAYONNAISE
SALT AND FRESHLY GROUND
   BLACK PEPPER

Mix all the ingredients together for a
lovely, simple colourful slaw.

REFRIED BEANS

AN EASY TO PUT TOGETHER
VEGETABLE OPTION TO TOP YOUR
BURGER – GREAT COMBINED WITH
GRATED CHEESE AND SLICED
TOMATOES.

1 TABLESPOON OLIVE OIL
½ ONION, SLICED
2 GARLIC CLOVES, FINELY
   CHOPPED
100G CAN BORLOTTI BEANS,
   DRAINED
100G CAN KIDNEY BEANS,
   DRAINED
100G CAN BLACK BEANS, DRAINED
1 TABLESPOON TOMATO PURÉE

Heat the oil in a frying pan over a
medium heat. Add the onion and garlic
and fry until softened. Add the beans
and tomato purée and cook for about
8 minutes over a medium heat or until
the beans begin to split and go to mush,
creating almost a bean paste!

BARBECUED WHOLE SEA BREAM WITH LEMON, FENNEL & GARLIC

I always find cooking a whole fish on the barbie to be such an occasion.
It looks stunning when presented on a bed of lovely fresh mixed salad or
spinach leaves and tastes of a Mediterranean summer's evening. Serves 2

1 FENNEL BULB, FINELY CHOPPED
½ RED ONION, FINELY CHOPPED
3 GARLIC CLOVES, CRUSHED
ZEST OF 1 LEMON
ZEST OF 1 ORANGE
6 ANCHOVIES, IN OLIVE OIL,
   DRAINED AND CHOPPED
1 TABLESPOON CAPERS IN BRINE,
   DRAINED
1 TABLESPOON CRACKED
   BLACK PEPPER
BUNCH OF DILL
BUNCH OF TARRAGON
1 ORANGE, SLICED
2 WHOLE SEA BREAM,
APPROXIMATELY 500G EACH,
   GUTTED, SCALED AND CLEANED
20ML OLIVE OIL

First soak 8 pieces of string in water – they are used to
keep the filling in place and this stops them from burning
during cooking!

Place the fennel, onion, garlic, lemon and orange zests,
anchovies, capers and pepper in a mixing bowl and
combine well. Arrange the dill and tarragon sprigs and
orange slices in the fish cavities and then stuff with the
fennel mixture. As the fish is exposed to the heat, the
juices from the orange, lemons and herbs will begin to
steam the fish from the inside, making this a super-fresh
delight! Once the cavities are filled, tie 4 pieces of string
around each fish.

Drizzle the olive oil over the fish, before cooking on the
preheated barbecue for around 7 minutes on each side.
Be careful not to let the fish stick to the grill rack as it
becomes beautiful and delicate.

WHOLE SCALLOPS IN THEIR SHELLS

I've done a fair few posh barbecues in my time, and this dish never fails to please. You need to buy really fresh scallops in the shell and if you can afford some hand-dived beauties, then go for it! Cooking the scallop in the shell will give you every bit of that fresh 'sea' flavour we need. Serves 4

4 SCALLOPS, IN THE SHELL
PINCH OF PAPRIKA
10G BUTTER
1 GARLIC CLOVE, FINELY
  CHOPPED
½ RED CHILLI, DESEEDED AND
FINELY DICED
PINCH OF SZECHUAN PEPPER
SMALL BUNCH OF FRESH
CORIANDER, LEAVES AND STALKS
  FINELY CHOPPED
SALT

Preheat the oven to 150°C/gas mark 2. Line a baking tray with baking parchment.

Remove the roes (the orange bit), muscles and main scallop from the shell, and set the scallop aside. Discard the muscles, and place the roes on the lined tray with a pinch of salt and the paprika. Bake in the oven for 3 hours, or until dry. Blitz up in a food processor to a powder and you have a delicious scallop garnish!

To cook the scallops, place the empty shells on the preheated barbecue, until they begin to get hot. Add one-quarter of the butter, garlic and chilli to each shell and leave on the barbecue until it begins to smoke. Sear the scallops in the shells for 2 minutes on each side, until caramelised on both sides, and place in a bowl ready to serve.

Sprinkle over some Szechuan pepper, a pinch of the dried scallop roe and some fresh coriander to serve.

CORN ON THE COB WITH SPICY CAJUN BUTTER

Everybody loves a good old corn on the cob on the barbie. From kids to the colonel, it's a winner for all and is a lovely side to a usually protein-heavy barbecue! For speed, I always blanch my corn first, and then finish it off on the barbie for that great smoky flavour. Serves 6

3 CORN ON THE COB, LEAVES AND STRANDS REMOVED AND HALVED
1 TEASPOON CUMIN SEEDS
1 TEASPOON FENNEL SEEDS
2 TABLESPOONS OLIVE OIL
1 RED ONION, FINELY CHOPPED
½ RED CHILLI, DESEEDED AND FINELY DICED
1 GARLIC CLOVE, CRUSHED
1 TABLESPOON SMOKED PAPRIKA
1 TABLESPOON CAYENNE PEPPER
1 TABLESPOON BLACK TREACLE
150G UNSALTED BUTTER, AT ROOM TEMPERATURE
SALT AND FRESHLY GROUND BLACK PEPPER

There are quite a few ingredients to make this butter, but believe me, it's worth it!

Firstly, bring a large pan of salted water to the boil. Drop in the corn and blanch on a high heat for about 10 minutes before removing from the pan and patting dry on some kitchen paper.

In the meantime, crack on to this Cajun butter bad boy! Dry fry the cumin and fennel seeds in a medium frying pan over a medium heat for 4–5 minutes or until fragrant. Set aside.

Heat the oil in the same frying pan over a medium heat, and cook the red onion, chilli and garlic until softened. Once cooked, add 100ml water, and all the remaining ingredients, apart from the butter. Once the water has almost fully reduced and the mixture begins to thicken, remove the pan from the heat and blitz the mixture in a food processor. Slowly add the butter until it's fully combined.

Spread the butter all over the corn. Place on the preheated barbie, and continue to baste in the butter until you get a lovely charred colour all over the cob. Add a little more seasoning if necessary, and get both hands on either side, don't be shy – just tuck in!

LOBSTER BURGERS WITH THERMIDOR SAUCE

This is the other half to our Burgers and Bordeaux evening. Tasty and ever-so-slightly decadent, it nevertheless won't break the bank. I've used Atlantic prawns as the patty base, with chunks of lobster in there too, for good measure. It's served with a thick thermidor-style sauce which is actually more of a roux, since the thicker sauce allows it to sit better on the burger and not make it so messy. Serves 4

FOR THE SAUCE
75G BUTTER
1 SHALLOT, DICED
150ML WHITE WINE
   (PREFERABLY BORDEAUX)
50G PLAIN FLOUR
150ML SEMI-SKIMMED MILK
50G GRUYÈRE CHEESE, GRATED
BUNCH OF CURLY LEAF PARSLEY,
   FINELY CHOPPED

FOR THE BURGERS
2 LOBSTER TAILS,
   APPROXIMATELY 225G EACH
30ML OLIVE OIL
100G BANANA SHALLOTS,
   FINELY CHOPPED
2 GARLIC CLOVES,
   FINELY CHOPPED
400G COOKED, PEELED PRAWNS,
   DICED
40G COARSE, WHITE, DRIED
   BREADCRUMBS, PLUS EXTRA
   IF NECESSARY
JUICE OF 1 LEMON
3 SPRIGS OF PARSLEY,
   FINELY CHOPPED
2 RED PEPPERS, DESEEDED
   AND DICED
4 BRIOCHE BUNS, SPLIT,
   TO SERVE

Melt 25g of the butter in a small pan and fry the shallot until softened. Add the white wine, bring to the boil, then lower the heat and simmer until the liquid is reduced by half. Place to one side.

Melt the remaining butter in a medium pan set over a medium heat. Stir in the flour and cook, stirring constantly for a couple of minutes. Slowly add the milk, whisking as you do, to prevent the sauce from becoming lumpy. Add the cheese, parsley and the reduced wine and shallot sauce. This should sit nicely on the burger as it oozes from the bun!

Preheat the oven to 180°C/gas mark 4.

Place the lobster tails on a baking tray and drizzle with 15ml of the oil. Cook in the oven for 8 minutes. Once cooked, submerge in cold water, to stop the cooking process, and make them cool enough to handle.

Using a sharp kitchen knife, turn the lobster tail over (so as it's on its back), and make two cuts down either side of the tail. Pull the middle part of the underbelly out before pulling the sides of the shell apart, making it easy to pull out the tail. And voila!

Pour the remaining olive oil into a frying pan set over a medium heat and fry the banana shallots and garlic for 3–4 minutes. Blitz the prawns in a blender, then add the cooked shallots and garlic, breadcrumbs, lemon juice and parsley and, of course, the big daddy lobster, cut into small chunks. The consistency of the burger should be a smooth patty with small chunks of lobster and diced shallots! If the mixture is a little too moist, add more breadcrumbs until it binds.

Shape the mixture into 4 equal-sized bad boy patties using a 7cm ring cutter, or your fine hands will do! Place on a baking tray lined with baking parchment, season with salt and pepper and cook for 12 minutes.

Whilst they're in the oven, place the pepper chunks on a griddle pan set over a medium heat. Cook for around 2–3 minutes on each side, until nicely coloured.

To serve, place a burger on the base of each bun, followed by the peppers and a dollop of the thermidor sauce, top with the brioche halves and indulge!

SPECIAL MEALS

FIG, GOAT CURD & PROSCIUTTO SALAD WITH CHORIZO & HONEY DRESSING

This is a great, quick-fire salad and is super-colourful, too! I much prefer goat curd to goat's cheese – it's a lighter, less intimidating, alternative and is great for salads.
Serves 6

120G PINE NUTS
100G ROCKET
6 FRESH FIGS, QUARTERED
180G PROSCIUTTO, FINELY SLICED
200G GOAT CURD (AVAILABLE
 FROM MOST GOOD DELIS AND
 CHEESE COUNTERS)
SEA SALT

FOR THE DRESSING
75ML CHORIZO OIL (SEE PEA AND
 MINT VELOUTÉ ON PAGE 162)
40ML SHERRY VINEGAR
2 TEASPOONS GOOD-QUALITY
 CLEAR HONEY

Preheat the oven to 150°C/gas mark 2. Toast the pine nuts on a baking tray in the oven for 15 minutes.

Meanwhile, arrange the rocket leaves over a large serving dish and sit the fig quarters in rows along the dish. Lay the prosciutto slices over the top of the figs and spoon the goat curd around them. Scatter the toasted pine nuts over the salad.

To make the dressing, combine all the ingredients in a bowl using a whisk and drizzle over the salad. Sprinkle a little sea salt over the top and you're good to go!

SEARED SCALLOPS & SPICED CAULIFLOWER PURÉE

This dish is a banger, and probably my favourite to eat. Big juicy scallops, served with sweet pancetta, a lightly spicy cauliflower purée with a walnut crumb and truffle-cured beetroot. It's pretty quick to prep, and goes down a storm. We did it as a starter at Britain's first gay wedding and although it's easy to prep for a small dinner party, it takes little longer when you're doing it for 70... Serves 4

50G CUBED PANCETTA
100ML MAPLE SYRUP
50G WALNUTS
150G SMALL CAULIFLOWER
   FLORETS
200ML SEMI-SKIMMED MILK
SMALL PINCH OF GROUND CUMIN
SMALL PINCH OF MEDIUM
   CURRY POWDER
1 RAW BEETROOT
15ML TRUFFLE OIL, PLUS EXTRA
   FOR DRIZZLING
8 SCALLOPS
KNOB OF BUTTER
MALDON SEA SALT AND FRESHLY
   GROUND BLACK PEPPER

First things first, marinate the pancetta cubes in maple syrup, and allow them to gather flavour for at least 1 hour – overnight, if possible.

Preheat the oven to 150°C/gas mark 2.

Place the marinated pancetta on a baking tray, and bake for around 30 minutes, until the pancetta becomes sticky and crispy.

Meanwhile, place the walnuts on a separate baking tray and toast in the oven for around 15 minutes. Allow them to cool, and then crush to a coarse rubble to make the walnut crumb. Easy!

To make the purée, place the cauliflower florets in a medium saucepan and cover with the milk. Add the cumin and curry powder. Bring to the boil, reduce to simmer and cook until the cauliflower is tender, for around 15 minutes, then blend to a purée using a hand-held electric blender. Season to taste.

To prepare the beetroot (this is really easy) just cut the beetroot really thinly (with a mandolin if you have one), drizzle with a dash of truffle oil, sprinkle Maldon sea salt over the top, and cover for at least 1 hour – the salt and oil will cook/cure it slightly.

Finally, all that's left to do is to sear the scallops, and plate up. Place the truffle oil in a heavy frying pan, along with the butter. Get the pan really hot before putting the scallops in, so you get a really nice caramel sear, and cook for around 40 seconds on each side.

Now all that's left is to plate up! Spoon a dollop of purée onto each plate and top with the scallops. Delicately place the beetroot around the scallops before scattering the whole thing with the pancetta and walnuts.

SWORDFISH CEVICHE

I used to serve this delicious zingy and summery dish – an oriental twist on a South American classic – when I was a chef on private yachts. Really simple, amazing fresh fish packed with a punch of coriander. We used to have access to incredible ingredients straight from the sea which made it onto the plate within a few hours. Serves 4

FOR THE COLA AND SOY REDUCTION
500ML COLA
50ML SOY SAUCE

FOR THE PEPPER PURÉE
2 RED PEPPERS, DESEEDED AND
  ROUGHLY CHOPPED
100ML OLIVE OIL
PINCH OF CHILLI POWDER

FOR THE CEVICHE
800G SWORDFISH STEAK, CUT INTO
  1CM CHUNKS
BUNCH OF CORIANDER,
  FINELY CHOPPED
3 BEEF TOMATOES, DESEEDED
  AND FINELY DICED
½ RED ONION, FINELY DICED
JUICE OF 5 LIMES
50G WASABI PEAS, CRUSHED
SALT AND FRESHLY GROUND
  BLACK PEPPER

Place the ingredients for the reduction in a small pan, bring to the boil, then turn down the heat to a simmer for about 45 minutes to an hour, allowing the liquid to reduce by about 90 per cent until it becomes syrupy.

For the purée, place all the ingredients in another small pan. Place on a low heat and allow the peppers to slowly cook in the olive oil until soft, about 30 minutes. Then, using a slotted spoon, transfer the peppers to a blender and blend, at the same time slowly adding the oil until you have a smooth and shiny purée.

For the ceviche, place the fish, coriander, tomato and onion in a mixing bowl, season and cover with lime juice. Chill for 45 minutes until the flesh of the swordfish goes from raw to opaque. Essentially, the acids in the lime juice will have just cooked the fish.

To plate up, place a 5cm cutter on a serving plate. Drain the ceviche mix and place ¼ of the mixture in the cutter then remove the cutter. Place dots of purée and soy reduction around the plate and sprinkle with the crushed wasabi peas. Repeat for each serving.

CHICKEN LIVER PARFAIT WITH BRIOCHE SOLDIERS

This to me is a winner in so many ways. The parfait is rich, smooth and silky, with a deep flavour, and the other elements complement it really well – sharp cornichons, sweet chutney, crunchy chicken skin and some lovely toast to spread it on. Serves 8

FOR THE PARFAIT

2 SHALLOTS, ROUGHLY CHOPPED
2 GARLIC CLOVES, CRUSHED
3 SPRIGS OF THYME
SPRIG OF SAGE
SPRIG OF ROSEMARY
1 BAY LEAF
200ML PORT OR GOOD RED WINE
50ML BRANDY
400G CHICKEN LIVERS, DRAINED
    AND PATTED DRY WITH
    KITCHEN PAPER
6 MEDIUM EGGS
400G BUTTER, MELTED
SALT AND FRESHLY GROUND
    BLACK PEPPER

FOR THE CRISPY CHICKEN SKIN

8 PIECES CHICKEN SKIN,
    EACH ABOUT 8-10CM LONG
MALDON SEA SALT

FOR THE CHUTNEY

20ML VEGETABLE OIL
30G BUTTER
1 RED ONION, THINLY SLICED
SPLASH OF PORT
2 TABLESPOONS BALSAMIC
    VINEGAR
2 TABLESPOONS SUGAR
1 CINNAMON STICK
1 STAR ANISE
1 BAY LEAF

TO SERVE

8 SLICES BRIOCHE
XX CORNICHONS, FINELY CHOPPED

Preheat the oven to 150°C/gas mark 2. Line an 18cm loaf tin with greaseproof paper, leaving enough to overlap at the top.

Place the shallots, garlic, herbs, port and brandy in a saucepan, and reduce over a high heat until reduced by a third. This ensures the flavours infuse into the liquid and burns off the booze!

In a blender, whizz up the raw livers, and add the reduced alcohol mix. Continue to blitz until smooth, slowly adding the eggs, one at a time, followed by the melted butter – it's important not to rush this as if you do the mixture can separate and, once it's gone, it's gone!

Season the mixture, then pass through a fine sieve to eliminate any lumps or herb sprigs, leaving you with a really smooth parfait mix.

Spoon the parfait mix into the loaf tin, then place the loaf tin in a roasting tin. Add 1.5 litres of boiling water to the roasting tin, and then cover everything with foil. Cooking this bad boy au bain marie helps ensure it bakes evenly. Place in the oven for around 40 minutes or until the centre of the parfait reaches over 62°C on a meat probe. If you don't have a probe, it's all about the wobble. There should be a very slight wobble in the middle before removing.

Allow to cool for 4 hours in the fridge before placing on to a chopping board and cutting into lovely slices that can stand on the plate.

Whilst the parfait is cooling, crack on with the crispy chicken skin. This is a great garnish on lots of dishes, and goes really well with so many things... try it on a scallop dish too! I used to dry these out at the bottom of the oven for blooming hours and days until someone showed me a much quicker and easier way.

Preheat the oven to 200°C/gas mark 6. Line a baking tray with baking parchment.

Lay the skin out flat on a chopping board and, using a sharp knife, scrape all the excess fat from the skin. Spread out on the lined tray and season well with salt. Place another sheet of baking parchment and a tray on top (this keeps the chicken skin from crinkling, giving you a large 'shard'-like appearance), and bake for around 25 minutes or until crispy and golden.

For the chutney, heat the oil and butter in a medium pan over a medium heat and fry the onion. Once softened, add the port and balsamic vinegar, along with the sugar, cinnamon stick, star anise (which is what makes this!) and bay leaf. Allow all of the moisture to reduce, and continue to stir to stop it from catching. Set aside.

Now put everything together. Toast the brioche. Stand a slice of parfait up on its side. Add a quenelle of the chutney (another posh chef term for an oval shaped using two spoons), and sprinkle the chopped cornichons round the plate. Stand a shard of chicken skin up against the parfait, and there you have it!

TOMATO & LEMON CURED HAKE WITH TOMATO CONSOMMÉ

This is a lovely, delicate-looking starter, ideal for a summer's evening. It's undoubtedly the tomatoes that make the dish, so you'll need to get some well-grown, super-fresh ripe tommies and some muslin cloth for this one. This needs a bit of preparation ahead of time. Serves 4

FOR THE HAKE
2 X 200G HAKE FILLETS
2 TABLESPOONS BLACK
  PEPPERCORNS
50G GRANULATED SUGAR
50G MALDON SEA SALT
SMALL BUNCH OF BASIL
2 TABLESPOONS VODKA
2 TOMATOES, BLENDED
JUICE OF 2 LEMONS

FOR THE TOMATO CONSOMMÉ
2KG TOMATOES
SMALL BUNCH OF BASIL
2 TABLESPOONS TARRAGON
  VINEGAR
2 TABLESPOONS VODKA
½ GARLIC CLOVE

FOR THE BEETROOT
12 BABY BEETROOT
100G CASTER SUGARD
1 STAR ANISE
2 CLOVES
1 BAY LEAF
150ML WHITE WINE VINEGAR
1 TEASPOO MUSTARD SEEDS
6 BLACK PEPPERCORNS
1 ALL SPICE BERRY

FOR THE GRANOLA
3 TABLESPOONS CRUSHED
  WALNUTS
3 TABLESPOONS CRUSHED
  CASHEWS
2 TABLESPOONS PINE NUTS
1 TABLESPOON PUMPKIN
  SEEDS
4 TABLESPOONS OATS
1 TABLESPOON CLEAR HONEY
2 EGG WHITES
2 TABLESPOONS OLIVE OIL
1 TEASPOON DRIED OREGANO
1 TEASPOON FRESH THYME
1 TEASPOON SNIPPED
  FRESH CHIVES
MALDON SEA SALT AND
  FRESHLY GROUND
  BLACK PEPPER

TO SERVE
8 SPINACH LEAVES PER
  PERSON
SPLASH OF EXTRA VIRGIN
  OLIVE OIL
PINCH SEA SALT

First cure the hake, it needs at least 24 hours, preferably 48. Lay one of the hake fillets on a piece of clingfilm, skin-side down. Mix the remaining ingredients together in a small bowl, and pour the mix over the top of the hake fillet. Place the other fillet on top, flesh side down, and then tightly wrap the fish in the clingfilm, but try to keep it relatively flat. Place in a roasting tray and place a heavy weight on top of the parcel. Rotate the fish every 12 hours. Once cured, scrape off the cure mixture, remove the skin and cut the flesh into long, thin strips.

For the tomato consommé, place all of the ingredients in a bowl and blitz with a hand-held blender. Spoon the mixture into a large piece of muslin and tie up tight, then suspend over a large bowl and allow it to drip into the bowl beneath. Ideally, leave overnight, or for at least 12 hours. What you should have in the morning is a light, delicious flavour of tomato. The liquid will be clear, but the flavour banging! Chill until ready to serve.

Next up, pickle the beets! Preheat the oven to 180°C/gas mark 4 and roast the beets for 40 minutes. Meanwhile, combine the remaining ingredients in a saucepan and bring to the boil to dissolve the sugar. Peel the cooked beetroots and place them in a jar along with the pickling vinegar. Leave the beetroot to pickle overnight. They'll keep for a good while, at least 2 weeks.

The next day, preheat the oven to 150°C/gas mark 2. Line a baking tray with greaseproof paper.

Right, finally for the savoury granola – this is a great addition and can add lots of texture to many a dish! Combine all of the ingredients together in a mixing bowl, season well and lay out on the baking tray. Bake for about 40 minutes or until the mix is golden, and little clusters form. Set aside to cool.

While the granola is baking, brush the spinach leaves with a little olive oil, sprinkle with sea salt and set aside ready to serve.

To plate up, place the beets and oiled spinach in the middle of the bowl, and sit the hake pieces on top, with about 5 tablespoons of the chilled tomato consommé in the bowl, and the savoury granola over the top of the hake. Deelishy fishy!

ROAST MALLARD, DIPS, ENDIVE, & PRAWN TOAST

This is a little twist on a chinese takeaway night in! We've got some pancakes with a shredded mallard, endive, spring onion and cucumber with a prawn toast starter. Buy your mallard from any good butchers and use really thin, ready made pancakes for an authentic takeaway feel! For the prawn toast recipe, see page 163. Serves 2–3.

1 PLUMP WILD DUCK

FOR THE PASTE
100G ONION, FINELY CHOPPED
1 GARLIC CLOVE
1 SPRIG THYME, LEAVES
  PICKED OFF
1 SPRIG ROSEMARY,
  LEAVES PICKED OFF
1 TABLESPOON FRESH
  CORRIANDER, CHOPPED
1 BAY LEAF
1 CLOVE
3 TABLESPOONS 5 SPICE POWDER

OLIVE OIL
ZEST AND JUICE OF 1/2 ORANGE
30G SOFT BROWN SUGAR
1 TABLESPOON BALSAMIC VINEGAR
2 TABLESPOONS DARK SOY SAUCE
20ML KETCHUP
1 TEASPOON WORCHESTER SAUCE
50ML APPLE JUICE

FOR THE PANCAKES
STEAMED PANCAKES
½ CUCUMBER, FINELY CHOPPED
1 ENDIVE
2 SPRING ONIONS

Blitz all of the paste ingredients in a food processor, and blend to a fine paste. Add a splash of olive oil to a saucepan and fry the paste over a medium heat for 2 minutes, before adding the remaining ingredients. Allow to simmer for 20 minutes.

Blend in the food processor again and then pass through a fine sieve. This sauce will be for our pancakes, but also our marinade.

Preheat the oven to 200°C/gas mark 6.

Take the mallad and prick with a fork all over, then rub all over with two thirds of the sauce. Place the mallard on its side in a roasting tray and roast for 30-40 minutes, basting the bird every 10 minutes or so. After 20 minutes turn the bird over on its other side. Remove from the oven and allow to rest for 10 minutes.

Now get pancaking! To serve, use two forks to shred the meat from the bone. Hold the mallard with one fork and scrape with the other to effectively shred the meat. Place on a plate, pile up the pancakes on a separate plate, put the hoisin sauce and salad ingredients in separate little bowls, and you're away! A gourmet night in front of the telly.

VENISON CARPACCIO WITH CHOCOLATE & BALSAMIC DRESSING

This is a simple dish that allows the flavour of a good venison fillet to shout out. I'm a huge fan of venison – the rich, gamey meat goes really well with chocolate. It's served with fresh orange segments which cuts through the richness of the meat beautifully. Serves 4

FOR THE VENISON
2 TABLESPOONS JUNIPER BERRIES
2 TABLESPOONS BLACK
   PEPPERCORNS
2 TABLESPOONS HERBES DE
   PROVENCE
1 TABLESPOON MALDON SEA SALT
400G VENISON LOIN
2 TABLESPOONS OLIVE OIL

FOR THE DRESSING
20G DARK CHOCOLATE
2 TABLESPOONS BALSAMIC
   VINEGAR
2 TABLESPOONS OLIVE OIL

TO SERVE
50G ROCKET
1 FENNEL BULB, STEMS
   FINELY CHOPPED
15ML EXTRA VIRGIN OLIVE OIL
2 ORANGES, EACH CUT INTO
   6 SEGMENTS
50G TOASTED FLAKED ALMONDS

Crush the juniper berries, peppercorns, herbs and salt using a pestle and mortar. Rub the mixture over the venison loin, cover and set aside in the fridge for 1 hour.

Heat the oil in a medium non-stick frying pan over a high temperature. Make sure the pan is really hot to allow for the venison to get a crust quickly when seared. Sear the loin well on all sides, and once it's coloured all over, set aside to cool.

For carpaccio, the venison fillets need to be nice and thin. Cut the slices off the fillet as thinly as possible, aiming for around 4 slices per person. Rest a few slices at a time on a piece of clingfilm on a chopping board, with plenty of space between each slice, then place another piece of clingfilm over the top, and with a rolling pin, bash the pieces down so they become super thin. Repeat to flatten all the slices.

Melt the dark chocolate in a heatproof bowl over a small pan of simmering water, before pouring in the balsamic vinegar and olive oil, stirring well to combine.

To serve, arrange the pieces of venison flat on the plates. Put a handful of rocket and fennel with a splash of olive oil, in a pile in the middle of the plate, and then place three orange segments around the sides of the plate, scatter over the toasted almonds, and a cheeky drizzle of the warm dressing – only a small amount – and there you have it!

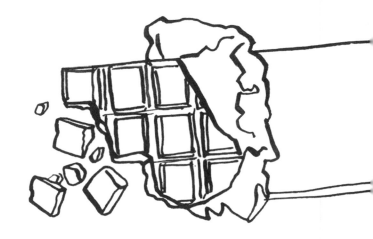

SPICED PEAR & BLUE CHEESE WINTER SALAD WITH TRUFFLE DRESSING

This is a lovely, colourful salad, quick to rustle up and tasty to eat! Serves 4

FOR THE SPICED PEARS
2 PEARS, CUT INTO LARGE
   WEDGES
200ML RED WINE
3 TABLESPOONS ORANGE JUICE
1 CINNAMON STICK
PINCH OF GROUND NUTMEG
1 STAR ANISE
1 CLOVE
1 BAY LEAF
50G BROWN GRANULATED SUGAR

FOR THE SALAD
50G WALNUTS
100G LAMB'S LETTUCE
1 CARROT, CUT INTO RIBBONS
   WITH A RIBBON PEELER
1 COOKED BEETROOT, CUT
   INTO WEDGES
¼ RED ONION, FINELY SLICED
10 RADISHES, HALVED
250G BLUE CHEESE (ROQUEFORT
   IS A WINNER WITH THIS ONE),
   CRUMBLED

FOR THE DRESSING
2 TABLESPOONS TRUFFLE OIL
1 TABLESPOON WHITE BALSAMIC
   VINEGAR
1 TABLESPOON CLEAR HONEY
SALT AND FRESHLY GROUND
   BLACK PEPPER

Preheat the oven to 150°C/gas mark 2.

Place all the ingredients for the spiced pears in a small pan over a low heat and simmer for 45 minutes or until the pears are purple and tender.

Place the walnuts on a baking tray, and toast in the oven for around 15 minutes. Set aside to cool.

Whisk the dressing ingredients together in a small jug.

Combine the salad ingredients and pears in a salad bowl, pour over the dressing and there you go! Who says salads are a summer thing, eh?!

FEAST FOR A (RICH) KING!

We've catered this menu as a main course for a couple of weddings, and it is indeed fit for a king! We've also combined all these dishes together for a Christmas party before and they've never failed to be a winning combo. It shouldn't take too long to do either, so let's crack on! Just remember to unbuckle your belt before you tuck in. Serves 8

MUSHROOMS

1 TABLESPOON TRUFFLE OIL
3 SHALLOTS, FINELY DICED
1 GARLIC CLOVE, CRUSHED
2 LARGE COOKED BEETROOTS,
  FINELY DICED
6 PORTOBELLO MUSHROOMS
2 TABLESPOONS DRIED THYME
300G BLUE CHEESE

To make the mushrooms, heat the oil over a medium heat in a small frying pan and sauté the shallots and garlic for 3 minutes, or until softened. Add the cooked beetroots for 3–4 minutes, then divide the mixture between the upturned mushrooms. Sprinkle with the thyme, then top with the blue cheese. Set to one side on a baking tray, ready to bake for 15 minutes at 180°C/gas mark 4 just before serving.

TOMATOES PROVENÇAL

3 LARGE BUFFALO TOMATOES,
  HALVED
3 TABLESPOONS DRIED OREGANO
SALT AND FRESHLY GROUND
  BLACK PEPPER
DRIZZLE OF OLIVE OIL

To make the tomatoes, place the tomato halves, cut-side up, on a baking tray and sprinkle over all the other ingredients. Bake with the mushrooms for 15 minutes.

PARMENTIER POTATOES

50G BUTTER
2 TEASPOONS OLIVE OIL
2 POTATOES, PEELED AND CUBED
½ ONION, FINELY CHOPPED
2 SPRIGS OF ROSEMARY, LEAVES
  PICKED AND FINELY CHOPPED
1 GARLIC CLOVE, CRUSHED
JUICE OF ½ LEMON
SALT AND FRESHLY GROUND
  BLACK PEPPER

Preheat the oven to 200°C/gas mark 6. To make the Parmentier potatoes, heat the butter and oil in a large frying pan over a medium heat, and cook the potatoes for 5 minutes, until golden. Add the onion, rosemary and garlic, and cook for a further 5 minutes. Pour over the lemon juice and seasoning, and transfer to a roasting tray. Roast for about 15 minutes.

ROCKET AND PARMESAN SALAD

100G ROCKET
75G PARMESAN SHAVINGS
DRIZZLE OF OLIVE OIL
SEA SALT

For the salad, combine the rocket and Parmesan, drizzle with a generous glug of oil and a pinch salt.

CHATEAUBRIAND

DRIZZLE OF VEGETABLE OIL
75G BUTTER
1KG TRIMMED FILLET STEAK,
  LEFT WHOLE
GENEROUS GRINDING OF SALT AND
  FRESHLY GROUND BLACK PEPPER

Preheat the oven to 200°C/gas mark 6. For the Chateaubriand, heat a large heavy-based frying pan over a high heat. Add the oil and butter, and allow the pan to get really hot. Add the fillet steak and sear all over, for about 5 minutes, until you get a lovely dark brown caramelisation around the meat. Tilt the pan and baste the juices over the meat. When you have a lovely colour all over, place the fillet on a roasting tray and cook in the oven for about 15 minutes, or until the centre is 58°C (use a kitchen thermometer). This will give you a lovely medium-rare Chateaubriand. Allow the meat to rest for at least 10 minutes before slicing at the table.

MONKFISH FILLET WITH RED PESTO & RATATOUILLE

I'm a huge fan of pesto with monkfish and ratatouille. A true taste of the Med! Serves 4

FOR THE PESTO ROSSO

100G SUN-DRIED TOMATOES, PLUS
    75ML OIL FROM THE JAR
50G TOASTED PINE NUTS
SMALL BUNCH OF BASIL
JUICE OF 1 LEMON
100G PARMESAN CHEESE, GRATED
1 GARLIC CLOVE
SALT AND FRESHLY GROUND
    BLACK PEPPER

FOR THE RATATOUILLE

20ML EXTRA VIRGIN OLIVE OIL
1 RED ONION, FINELY SLICED
1 GARLIC CLOVE, FINELY
    CHOPPED
1 RED PEPPER, DESEEDED
    AND CUT INTO LARGE CUBES
½ AUBERGINE, CUT INTO
    1CM CUBES
1 COURGETTE, CUT INTO
    HALF CIRCLES
75ML MARTINI ROSSO
100ML RED WINE
1 TABLESPOON TOMATO PURÉE
400G FRESH CHOPPED TOMATOES
1 BAY LEAF
SPRIG OF THYME
3 TABLESPOONS DRIED OREGANO

FOR THE BALLOTINES

2 COURGETTES, CUT INTO
    RIBBONS WITH A RIBBON
    PEELER
2 MONKFISH TAILS, ABOUT 800G
    TOTAL WEIGHT
20ML OLIVE OIL
1 TOMATO, FLESH DICED
BUNCH OF CURLY LEAF PARSLEY,
    CHOPPED
50G TOASTED PINE NUTS

For the pesto, blitz all of the ingredients in a food processor, season to taste, and there you have a pesto rosso! Set aside.

Heat the oil in a medium pan and fry the onion and garlic for 3–4 minutes or until softened. Once this is done, add the pepper and aubergine and continue to cook on a medium heat before adding the courgette about 5 minutes later.

After a couple of minutes, once all the vegetables begin to sweat, add the Martini Rosso (my secret weapon!), red wine, tomato purée, chopped tomatoes, bay leaf, thyme sprig and oregano. Simmer on a low heat for around 1 hour, until you get a lovely, rich tomatoey selection of stewed vegetables. Remove the thyme sprig and bay leaf.

Smother the monkfish fillet in the pesto rub around 1 hour before serving.

Next up, we're going to ballotine! This is a widely-used restaurant technique that helps to hold and set meats, fish and numerous other ingredients in clingfilm, making it neater and easier to cook. Place two 40cm pieces of clingfilm out flat on a work surface. Lay half the courgette ribbons flat onto each piece of clingfilm. Place each tail in the centre of the ribbons, and using the clingfilm for support, wrap the ribbons over the fish. Then roll the clingfilm away from your body, taking care to ensure there's no air trapped in the ballotine. Twist the sides of clingfilm, and tie a knot in either end … it's a little tricky, but with a few practices, you'll crack it!

Preheat the oven to 180°C/gas mark 4.

Bring a medium pan of water to the boil, add the ballotines and poach for 8 minutes in simmering water. Carefully remove the clingfilm and transfer to a baking tray. Bake in the oven for a further 6 minutes.

Cut the tails into medallions and sit them on top of a spoonful of ratatouille. Splash the olive oil over and serve with a sprinkle of diced tomato, chopped parsley and some toasted pine nuts.

BRAISED PORK BELLY, LOIN WRAPPED IN STREAKY BACON, APPLE PURÉE & MUSTARD MASH

This dish is one of my favourites. I love a good bit of pork! We did a variation of this dish for my Olympic 'Best of British Supper Club' and it doesn't get much more British than pork and apples. Serves 4

FOR THE PICKLED APPLES
500ML CIDER VINEGAR
100G GRANULATED SUGAR
1 THUMB-SIZED PIECE OF GINGER,
   PEELED AND SLICED
1 TEASPOON ALLSPICE BERRIES
1 TEASPOON WHOLE PEPPERCORNS
3 CINNAMON STICKS
2 STAR ANISE
12 SLICES OF GRANNY SMITH
   APPLES, CUT INTO BALLS
   WITH A MELON BALLER

FOR THE PORK BELLY
600G PORK BELLY, BONED
   AND SCORED
3 ONIONS, HALVED
2 CARROTS, ROUGHLY CHOPPED
1 CELERY STICK, ROUGHLY
   CHOPPED
2 GARLIC CLOVES, LEFT WHOLE
500ML CIDER
150ML PRESSED APPLE JUICE
1 BAY LEAF
2 SPRIGS OF THYME

FOR THE PORK TENDERLOIN
8 SLICES OF STREAKY BACON
400G PORK TENDERLOIN
1 GARLIC CLOVE, MINCED
2 TABLESPOONS FINELY CHOPPED
   SAGE LEAVES
SALT AND FRESHLY GROUND
   BLACK PEPPER
KNOB OF BUTTER
DRIZZLE OF OIL

FOR THE MASH
600G DESIREE POTATOES,
   PEELED AND QUARTERED
150G BUTTER
SPLASH OF MILK
SALT AND FRESHLY GROUND
   BLACK PEPPER
1 TEASPOON WHOLEGRAIN MUSTARD

FOR THE APPLE PURÉE
(SEE RECIPE ON PAGE 47)

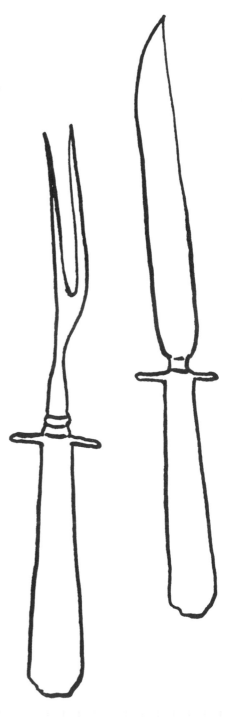

First of all, let's get the apples pickled. Place all the ingredients into a medium saucepan along with 250ml cold water and bring to the boil. Simmer for 5 minutes or until the tip of a sharp knife inserted into the apples is met with slight resistance. Set aside and allow to cool.

The next job is to get the pork belly done. Preheat the oven to 180°C/gas mark 4. Place the pork belly, onions, carrots, celery and garlic in a roasting tray along with the cider, apple juice, bay leaf and thyme. Cover with foil and roast for 2½ hours. After this time, increase the oven temperature to 230°C/gas mark 8, remove the foil and roast for a further 30 minutes – this way you get a lovely crispy crackling.

After the 3 hours, drain the cooking liquor into a saucepan, transfer the pork belly to a plate, wrap in greaseproof paper and place a weight on top to help get neat squares when portioning. Skim the fat off the liquor and reduce by half over a medium heat. All the cider, apple and pork belly juices will help to make a delicious sweet jus.

To prepare the pork tenderloin, place a large sheet of clingfilm on a work surface and lay the bacon slices over the top. Place the tenderloin perpendicularly on top of the bacon at one end and rub in the garlic, sage and seasoning before rolling the tenderloin in the streaky bacon, using the clingfilm to make a tight ballotine. Tie the ends securely and poach the ballotine in a large pan of simmering water for 12 minutes

Remove the ballotine from the pan, peel off the clingfilm and pan-fry in a hot pan with a knob of butter and a drizzle of oil, until the bacon becomes crispy and golden. Slice into 8 medallions.

About 25 minutes before plating up, make the mash. Boil the potatoes in a pan of boiling water. I like my potatoes really rich, so I go a bit mad on the butter. Once cooked, drain the potatoes in a colander, and while still hot, mash with the butter, milk, seasoning and mustard.

To serve, smear a circle of the apple purée in the centre of each plate and place all the components neatly on top of the purée, followed by a drizzle of the jus around the outside.

GUINEA FOWL & RISOTTO

I love making a good risotto. Who doesn't!? And with this one, we've found a way to make risotto look stunning so you can have restaurant-standard food at home. Serves 6

6 X GUINEA FOWL BREASTS, SKINS REMOVED AND RESERVED
4 TABLESPOONS OLIVE OIL
2 ONIONS, FINELY DICED
2 GARLIC CLOVES, FINELY CHOPPED
3 SPRIGS OF THYME, LEAVES FINELY CHOPPED
200G WILD MUSHROOMS (PORCINI OR WHATEVER'S IN SEASON)
400G PARMESAN CHEESE, FINELY GRATED
1 LITRE CHICKEN STOCK
KNOB OF BUTTER
1 CELERY STICK, FINELY CHOPPED
450G RISOTTO RICE E.G. ARBORIO
200ML WHITE WINE
JUICE OF 1 LEMON
200G SPINACH
SALT AND FRESHLY GROUND BLACK PEPPER

Make the guinea fowl skin crisps, following the instructions for crispy chicken skin on page 78.

Next make the guinea fowl ballotines: heat 2 tablespoons oil in a medium frying pan over a medium heat and add one-quarter of the diced onion, half the garlic and the thyme leaves. Season, and after a couple of minutes, add 100g of the mushrooms finely chopped. Once cooked, set to one side.

To stuff the breasts, with a small boning knife, pierce the breasts, lengthways, to make a long cavity about 1.5cm wide. Push the mushroom mix into the cavity of the breast. This can be a bit tricky, but it's worth the effort.

Next make the ballotines. Lay out a 40cm piece of clingfilm, place a stuffed guinea fowl breast at one end and season well. Overlap the clingfilm over the breast, and roll the clingfilm away from your body, taking care to ensure there's no air trapped in the ballotine. Twist the sides of clingfilm, and tie a knot in either end... just another 5 to do now! Set the ballotines aside to chill.

Next make the Parmesan crisps. Preheat the oven to 200°C/gas mark 6 and line a baking tray with greaseproof paper and place 6 round cutters on the tray. Divide 100g of the Parmesan cheese between the cutters, spreading it out to fill each one. Bake for 10 minutes (take care not to let them burn otherwise they'll taste awful!), and transfer to cool and set before peeling them off the greaseproof carefully.

Now let's crack on to the risotto. In one large pan, heat the chicken stock, and in another, add 2 tablespoons oil and the butter. Fry the remaining diced onion and garlic and the celery until they begin to soften. Add the risotto rice on a medium heat, and continue to move around the pan until the rice goes from being opaque to translucent. When this begins to happen, add the remaining mushrooms, roughly chopped, and continue to fry for a further 2 minutes before adding the white wine. Allow this to begin to reduce and turn the heat down, constantly stirring. As the moisture is absorbed, begin to add a ladleful at a time of the hot chicken stock, stirring constantly. Add the remaining Parmesan cheese, lemon juice and seasoning to the risotto, and continue to stir for around 20 minutes, or until the rice is al dente. Once the rice is cooked, stir in the spinach.

After you've been stirring the risotto for 12 minutes, bring a medium pan of water to the boil and poach the guinea fowl ballotines for 6 minutes. Once the guinea fowl is removed from the water, carefully remove the clingfilm.

To plate up, place a large spoonful of the risotto in 6 deep bowls, covering the whole base, then cut the ballotines into three, cutting the very ends off and discarding, and placing them like a triangle on the edge of the bowls. Stab the middle of the risotto with a couple of large shards of guinea fowl crisps and place the Parmesan circle leaning on one of the ballotines. Hope it looks (and tastes) as good as mine!

LAMB CANNON WITH HUMMUS PUREE & SWEET POTATO FONDANT

Lamb cannons need to be treated with the ultimate respect, mainly because they're pricey, but also because they're arguably the most sought-after part of the lamb. They're the inner, boneless eye of a lamb chop...good, eh? Serves 6

FOR THE LAMB JUS
1.5KG LAMB BONES
25ML VEGETABLE OIL
3 ONIONS, SKIN ON, HALVED
3 CARROTS, ROUGHLY CHOPPED
2 CELERY STICKS, CHOPPED
2 LEEKS, ROUGHLY CHOPPED
3 GARLIC CLOVES, ROUGHLY
  CHOPPED
1 TABLESPOON TOMATO PURÉE
100ML SWEET PORT
2 BAY LEAVES
4 SPRIGS OF THYME
SPRIG OF ROSEMARY

FOR THE CHARRED MED VEG
1 RED PEPPER, DESEEDED AND
  CUT INTO 8 SLICES
1 COURGETTE, CUT ON AN ANGLE
  INTO DISCS
25ML OLIVE OIL
SALT AND FRESHLY GROUND
  BLACK PEPPER

FOR THE HUMMUS PURÉE
50G HOMEMADE HUMMUS (PAGE 46)
JUICE OF 1 LEMON
100ML OLIVE OIL

FOR THE SWEET POTATO FONDANTS
25ML VEGETABLE OIL
125G BUTTER
4 PIECES OF SWEET POTATO,
  PEELED AND CUT INTO CYLINDERS
  WITH A 5CM CUTTER, 2-3CM DEEP
SPRIG OF ROSEMARY
1 GARLIC CLOVE
SPRIG OF THYME

FOR THE LAMB
3 LAMB CANNONS, APPROXIMATELY
300G EACH AND ABOUT 2CM THICK
VEGETABLE OIL
20G BUTTER
TOASTED FLAKED ALMONDS,
  TO GARNISH

Preheat the oven to 200°C/gas mark 6.

The first job to do is to get the stock underway. Place the bones in a roasting tin, and roast at the top of the oven for 45 minutes.

Meanwhile, heat the oil over a high heat in a large pan, and place the onion halves (still with skin on) flesh side down in the pot and allow to caramelise to a dark brown before adding the carrots, celery, leeks, garlic and tomato purée. Cook, moving the vegetables around until they begin to soften and caramelise on the bottom of the pan but not burn. Once done, add 20ml of the port and deglaze the pan.

Remove the roasted lamb bones from the oven and add them to the pan. The roasting tin should have some bits stuck to the bottom – these holds lots of flavour, so place the empty roasting tin on the hob, add the remaining port and scrape the bits away from the bottom before pouring the contents of the roasting tin into the pan. Cover the contents of the pan with water, add the herbs and bring to the boil, before reducing to a very low simmer. Allow the stock to reduce for as slow and as long as possible to give a super intense, delicious lamb jus.

After a couple of hours, skim the fat from the top of the pan (the clear liquid) and continue to reduce. After 6 hours (if you can wait that long!), strain the liquid, discard the bones and cooked veg and set 150ml to one side for the fondant potatoes. Place the remaining liquid into a clean pan, and continue to reduce over a low heat until the jus coats the back of a silver spoon when dunked...now that's a proper gravy.

Whilst the stock's simmering away, you've got plenty of time to crack on with all of the other bits.

Season the pepper and courgette. Heat the olive oil in a ridged griddle pan over a high heat, and let it get smoky (make sure the extractor's on). Sear the veg for about 3 minutes on each side, or until distinct lines appear on all sides.

For the hummus purée, place the hummus and lemon juice in a food processor and slowly drizzle in the olive oil until a smooth, swipeable consistency is reached.

For the sweet potato fondants the trick is plenty of butter, and a good stock! Put the oil in a deep frying pan, followed by the butter. Turn the heat up and add the seasoned potato cylinders. Keep turning until they begin to colour on each sides, then turn down the heat to medium, add the 150ml of reserved lamb stock, and the rosemary, garlic and thyme, and allow to cook for about 25 minutes, or until the potatoes are cooked through. Remove the fondants and transfer to a roasting tin ready to reheat later.

Preheat the oven to 200°C/gas mark 6.

Reheat the vegetables and fondants in the bottom of the oven while the lamb is cooking.

Finally, for the cannons. Heat a frying pan over a high heat with the oil and butter. Season the cannons before searing on all sides until they are a lovely dark colour all over, about 3 minutes on each side. Transfer to a roasting tin and roast for 6 minutes. Remove from the oven and set aside to rest, covered with foil. Each cannon should serve two, so cut into two nice medallions. It should be beautiful and pink.

To serve, create a circle of hummus purée in the middle of the plate and sit the pieces of lamb and fondants up on their side. Place the pieces of charred veg between the meat and potatoes and garnish with a sprinkle of toasted almonds and a drizzle of jus.

THAI-STYLE BEEF, MANGO & POMEGRANATE SALAD WITH CORIANDER & LIME DRESSING

The tropical fruit in this delicious – and very easy – salad adds a really fresh flavour that works well against ridiculously tender beef. I often serve it as a tiny canapé, but it's just as gorgeous and vibrant as a starter, snack or lunch. Serves 4

FOR THE MARINADE
2 TABLESPOONS SOY SAUCE
1 TABLESPOON NAM PLA
  (FISH SAUCE)
BUNCH OF FRESH CORIANDER,
STALKS AND LEAVES FINELY
  CHOPPED
JUICE OF 1 LIME
1 TABLESPOON SUGAR
1 TABLESPOON GROUND CINNAMON
1 TABLESPOON CHILLI POWDER
1 TABLESPOON GROUND CORIANDER
5CM PIECE OF FRESH ROOT
  GINGER, PEELED AND GRATED
1 MEDIUM CHILLI (OR HOT IF
  YOU PREFER!), DESEEDED AND
  FINELY CHOPPED
SALT AND FRESHLY GROUND
  BLACK PEPPER

FOR THE BEEF
1 BEEF CHEEK, TRIMMED AND
  CUT INTO 2CM CHUNKS
1 RED PEPPER, DESEEDED AND
  CUT INTO 1CM CHUNKS
1 ONION, ROUGHLY CHOPPED

FOR THE SALAD
4 LITTLE GEM LETTUCE, LEAVES
  SEPARATED
½ CUCUMBER, THINLY SLICED
1 RED PEPPER, DESEEDED
  AND SLICED
½ RED ONION, THINLY SLICED
1 MANGO, STONED AND DICED
200G CHERRY TOMATOES, HALVED
1 POMEGRANATE, HALVED AND
  SEEDS REMOVED
1 CARROT, CUT INTO RIBBONS
  WITH A RIBBON PEELER

TO GARNISH
10 MINT LEAVES, CHOPPED
SMALL BUNCH OF CORIANDER,
  CHOPPED
2 TABLESPOONS SOY SAUCE
JUICE OF 1 LIME
TSATZIKI (SEE PAGE 15),
  TO SERVE (OPTIONAL)

Place all the marinade ingredients in a non-metallic bowl and mix together. Then add the beef cheek, coat it thoroughly, cover and leave to marinate for a few hours in the fridge.

Preheat the oven to 150°C/gas mark 2.

Place the marinated beef cheek in a roasting tin with the pepper and onion and a splash of water. Cover with foil and cook for 3½ hours or until tender – you'll know when it's ready, as it will just fall apart when you press it. Remove from the oven and shred with a fork.

Divide the salad ingredients between 3 plates, top with the shredded beef, mint, coriander and a splash of soy sauce and lime juice… and there you have it!

If you're feeling the heat, perhaps serve this with a spoonful of homemade Tsatziki (see page 15).

RABBIT & APPLE SALAD WITH CIDER VINAIGRETTE

I made this dish over the summer at some big events, and it's a winner! One of my clients was having trouble with rabbits on his golf course, so we decided to do some pest control. We hunted the rabbits and used them for a gala dinner in France... true story! My grandma first got me trying rabbits in Spain as she used to breed them. I'll never forget when my sisters used to think they were pets, until they came back one day to find my grandma skinning them in the courtyard! It's fair to say she wasn't too popular with the Bugs Bunny-loving sisters that day! Serves 4

FOR THE PICKLED GIROLLES
150ML CIDER VINEGAR
80ML WATER
1 TEASPOON MUSTARD SEEDS
1 TEASPOON ALLSPICE BERRIES
2 BAY LEAVES
SPRIG OF THYME
100G FRESH GIROLLES

FOR THE RABBIT TERRINE
2 RABBIT LEGS (BACK LEGS)
250ML VEGETABLE OIL, PLUS
    EXTRA FOR FRYING
SPRIG OF THYME
SPRIG OF ROSEMARY
1 GARLIC CLOVE
1 CELERY STICK, FINELY DICED
½ CARROT, FINELY DICED
1 LEEK, FINELY DICED
75ML APPLE JUICE
2 GELATINE LEAVES, SOAKED
2 TABLESPOONS FRESH SAGE,
    FINELY CHOPPED
SALT AND FRESHLY GROUND
    BLACK PEPPER

FOR THE DRESSING
2 TABLESPOONS CIDER VINEGAR
1 TABLESPOON OLIVE OIL
1 TEASPOON CLEAR HONEY
1 TEASPOON WHOLEGRAIN MUSTARD

FOR THE LOINS AND BLACK PUDDING
KNOB OF BUTTER
2 RABBIT LOINS
150G BLACK PUDDING, CUT INTO
    SMALL CUBES

TO SERVE
APPLE PURÉE DIP (SEE PAGE 47)
HANDFUL OF PEA SHOOTS

Start by making the pickled girolles. Heat all the pickling ingredients, minus the girolles, in a small saucepan. Once the liquid comes to the boil, remove the pan from the heat and leave to cool for 3 minutes before adding the girolles. They'll take no time to cook and pickle, and we don't want to overcook them! Allow to cool and set aside so you can crack on with the other bits.

Preheat the oven to 120°C/gas mark ½. To make the rabbit terrine, place the rabbit legs, oil, thyme, rosemary and garlic in a roasting tin and roast for 5 hours.

In the meantime, heat a splash of oil in a frying pan and sauté the celery, carrot and leek for 6 minutes until almost cooked through, with the carrots still al dente, and set aside. Heat the apple juice in a small pan, drop in the soaked gelatine leaves and combine thoroughly.

After 5 hours, remove the rabbit legs from the roasting tin and allow to cool for 20 minutes on kitchen paper, then flake the meat into a bowl and mix lightly. Add the sautéed vegetables along with the sage, and season with salt and black pepper. Stir in the apple/gelatine mix and evenly spread the mixture onto a tray lined with clingfilm, then chill overnight in the fridge.

To make the dressing, place all the ingredients into a small bowl and whisk until combined.

To cook the loins, heat the butter in a frying pan over a high heat and pan-fry the loins for about 5 minutes. Set to one side and allow to rest for a further 5 minutes before cutting each into two pieces. In the same pan, fry the black pudding for 2 minutes on each side, and voilà!

Place a few dots of apple purée around each plate, a slice of the terrine in the middle, with a loin resting on top. Scatter the black pudding, pickled girolles and pea shoots around the edge of the plate and drizzle with the dressing. One of my favourites!

VENISON FILLET WITH PARSNIPS & PORT REDUCTION

I love cooking with game, I find hunting is the most authentic form of sourcing meat, so when I get a lovely piece of venison loin from my gamekeeping friend Rick, we give it the love it deserves. Serves 4

FOR THE PARSNIP PURÉE
2 PARSNIPS, PEELED AND CUT
   INTO CHUNKS
300ML SEMI-SKIMMED MILK
1 BAY LEAF
1 TEASPOON VANILLA EXTRACT
SALT AND FRESHLY GROUND
   BLACK PEPPER

FOR THE PARSNIP FONDANTS
30ML VEGETABLE OIL
100G BUTTER
2 PARSNIPS, SKIN ON,
   HALVED LENGTHWAYS
500ML BEEF STOCK
SPRIG OF THYME

FOR THE VENISON
800G VENISON LOIN, TRIMMED
   AND CLEANED
30ML TRUFFLE OIL
KNOB OF BUTTER
1 TABLESPOON CRANBERRY JELLY
200ML PORT
PARSNIP CRISPS (SEE PAGE 159
   FOR METHOD), TO SERVE

Place the parsnip chunks in a small pan over a medium heat, add the milk and bay leaf. Bring to the boil, then reduce to a simmer and cook for about 20 minutes or until the parsnips are softened and cooked through.

Remove the bay leaf. Transfer the parsnips and milk to a food processor and blitz until you get a lovely smooth consistency. Stir in the vanilla extract, and season, to taste.

For the parsnip fondants, put the oil in a deep frying pan, followed by the butter. Turn the heat up and add the seasoned parsnip halves. Keep turning until they begin to colour on each side, then turn down the heat to medium, add the stock and thyme, and you should get a lovely golden colour all over the parsnips after about 8 minutes!

Preheat the oven to 200°C/gas mark 6.

Season the loin generously before placing the truffle oil in a medium non-stick frying pan over a high heat. Sear the meat on all sides before transferring to the oven for around 12 minutes. Remove from the oven and set aside to rest for at least 10 minutes before slicing into 4 medallions.

Finally, take the frying pan, place it back on the heat and add the butter and cranberry jelly to the pan before deglazing the pan with the port. Allow to reduce for a couple of minutes to give a rich, sweet reduction for your dish.

Reheat the purée in a pan with a little milk, and the fondants in the oven for 15 minutes at 180°C/gas mark 4.

Serve with a circle of parsnip purée, the fondant on the outside with the parsnip crisps intertwined and the port reduction around the outside of the plate.

ORIENTAL CRAYFISH SALAD WITH RICE WINE & DRESSING

Crayfish is considered a huge pest in our waters, as the American Crayfish is eating much of our native river life, so it seems only right that we do our bit to control this pest by encouraging you to put it on your plate! Serves 6

FOR THE SALAD
200G BLACK RICE
200G MANGETOUT
100G DRIED EGG NOODLES
800G COOKED, PEELED
  CRAYFISH TAILS
½ CHINESE CABBAGE, SHREDDED
1 RED PEPPER, DESEEDED AND
  DICED INTO 1CM CUBES
2 SPRING ONIONS, FINELY
  CHOPPED
100G TOASTED FLAKED ALMONDS
2 CARROTS, CUT INTO RIBBONS
  WITH A RIBBON PEELER
1 CUCUMBER, CUT INTO RIBBONS
  WITH A RIBBON PEELER

FOR THE DRESSING
1 TABLESPOON FINELY CHOPPED
  FRESH CORIANDER
3 TABLESPOONS RICE WINE
  VINEGAR
2 TABLESPOONS SOY SAUCE
JUICE OF 1 LIME
5CM PIECE OF FRESH ROOT
  GINGER, PEELED AND GRATED
1 TEASPOON SUGAR
1 TABLESPOON OLIVE OIL

Preheat the oven to 180°C/gas mark 4.

Place the rice in a medium pan of boiling water and cook for 15 minutes or until soft and cooked. Drain and rinse with cold water. Set aside.

Meanwhile, blanch the mangetout in a pan of salted, boiling water for 4 minutes, and drain and rinse with cold water.

Place the noodles on a baking tray and bake them until golden brown. Leave them to cool and then crush them with your hands... I love these as a crunchy addition to a salad!

Combine all the dressing ingredients in a small jug, and whisk until thoroughly mixed.

Place all the salad ingredients in a large serving bowl and stir to combine. Add the dressing... badabing!

DESSERTS

ULTIMATE CHOCOLATE BROWNIES

These brownies are a favourite as an afternoon tea. You can add a drizzle of raspberry coulis, a dollop of ice cream and a nut crumb to transform them into a perfectly good dessert! This is an adaptation of my friend Marcus' recipe, and he's the finest cake man I know! Cuts into 13 squares

300G UNSALTED BUTTER
300G COCOA POWDER
500G CASTER SUGAR
1 TEASPOON VANILLA ESSENCE
8 MEDIUM EGGS
240G PLAIN CHOCOLATE, GRATED
200G PLAIN FLOUR
1 TABLESPOON BAKING POWDER

Preheat the oven to 160°C/gas mark 3. Line a deep baking tray – 22 x 18cm is best for a nice chunky brownie – with greaseproof paper.

Melt the butter in a large saucepan, then remove from the heat and stir in the cocoa powder, sugar, vanilla and eggs. Stir in the grated chocolate, flour and baking powder until fully combined. Pour the mix into the prepared tray and bake for about 45 minutes or until set with an ever-so-slight wobble. They will be lovely and moist once cooled!

CHOCOLATE MOUSSE WITH PEANUT BRITTLE & BANANA SPONGE

This is another winning combo – you just can't go wrong with peanuts and chocolate. The rich mousse is super quick and the sponge is a doddle to make, so what are you waiting for? Get cracking! Serves 4

FOR THE CHOCOLATE MOUSSE
115G DARK CHOCOLATE (50-70% COCOA SOLIDS, DEPENDING ON WHETHER YOU PREFER A SWEET OR BITTER MOUSSE), BROKEN INTO PIECES
4 LARGE EGGS, SEPARATED

FOR THE PEANUT BRITTLE
BUTTER, FOR GREASING
300G CASTER SUGAR
70G PEANUTS, CHOPPED
PINCH OF SALT·

FOR THE BANANA SPONGE
150G BUTTER
150G CASTER SUGAR
3 LARGE EGGS
2 MEDIUM OVERRIPE BANANAS, MASHED WITH A FORK
150G PLAIN FLOUR
1 TABLESPOON BAKING POWDER

For the mousse, place the chocolate in a medium heatproof bowl over a pan of simmering water (au bain marie) and stir occasionally until melted.

Meanwhile, in a separate medium bowl, whisk the egg whites until soft peaks form.

Once the chocolate has melted, stir in the egg yolks until fully combined and thick. Slowly fold the egg whites into the chocolate, using a tablespoon or spatula. Be careful to fold the mixture and not stir it, so you can keep all the air in the mousse, making it tastier and fluffier!

Once the egg whites are fully incorporated, place in a suitable container to set. I like to quenelle the mousse on to plates but if you think it may not hold, divide it equally between 4 individual serving dishes.

For the brittle, line a baking tray with foil and lightly butter it. Place 3 tablespoons of water and the sugar in a medium non-stick frying pan over a medium heat and allow the sugar to heat up. Stir until all the sugar has melted, and the mixture goes an amber colour. Remove from the heat, and add the chopped peanuts before spreading the mixture out on to the foil. Set aside to cool before breaking off big shards.

Preheat the oven to 160°C/gas mark 3. Grease and line a 15 x 22cm baking tray with baking parchment.

For the sponge, cream the butter and sugar together in a medium bowl before adding the eggs, followed by the bananas, and finally the flour and baking powder. Stir well to combine and transfer the mixture to the prepared tin. Bake for 1 hour or until a skewer comes out clean.

Allow to cool in the tray for 20 minutes and then transfer to a wire rack to cool completely. Cut the sponge into 2 x 8cm fingers.

To serve the pudding, make a large queinelle of chocolate mousse, sit the sponge fingers up against the queinelle and rest a large piece of peanut brittle sheet over the top of the mousse.

Any leftover sponge fingers should certainly be enjoyed with a good cup of tea and your feet up! Or clingfilm 'em up and they'll keep well for about 3 days … they also freeze well!

WINTER WONDERLAND

This dessert is one of my favourites in the run up to the crazy period. It's a fabulous combination of creamy white chocolate parfait with spiced pears topped with hazelnut crumb served with mulled wine syrup and blackberry coulis – you don't do as many ski seasons as I've done and not have a good spiced pear recipe (with a few extras to add on) up your sleeve! Serves 8

FOR THE PARFAIT
200G WHITE CHOCOLATE, BROKEN
   INTO PIECES
600ML DOUBLE CREAM
150G CASTER SUGAR
8 MEDIUM EGG YOLKS

FOR THE PEARS
8 PEARS
750ML RED WINE
250ML ORANGE JUICE
2 CINNAMON STICKS
2 STAR ANISE
1 WHOLE CLOVE
1 TEASPOON FRESHLY
   GRATED NUTMEG
4 TABLESPOONS BROWN SUGAR

FOR THE BLACKBERRY COULIS
250G FRESH OR FROZEN
   BLACKBERRIES
2 TABLESPOONS ICING SUGAR

FOR THE HAZELNUT CRUMB
50G HAZELNUTS, SKINNED
ORANGE SEGMENTS, TO DECORATE

Best to get the super easy parfait on the go first and into the freezer. Place the chocolate in a medium heatproof bowl over a pan of simmering water and stir occasionally, until melted.

Whip the cream to soft peaks and then set aside. Bring 100ml water and the sugar to the boil in a small pan, to create a sugar syrup. In a large bowl, whisk the egg yolks until pale and thick before whisking in the sugar syrup. Continue to whisk the mixture whilst adding in the melted chocolate, then quickly fold in the whipped cream. Pour the mixture into a 18 x 10cm terrine tin lined with clingfilm and freeze for at least 4 hours or until solid. Slice to serve.

Peel the pears, and slice off the bottoms. Stand the pears, upright, in a medium pan. Add the red wine, orange juice, cinnamon sticks, star anise, clove, nutmeg and 3 tablespoons of the brown sugar to the pan and simmer for 1½ hours or until the pears are cooked through. Keep warm while you make the coulis.

When the pears are cooked, spoon out about 200ml of the cooking liquid into a small pan and add the remaining brown sugar. Cook to reduce until a shiny mulled wine syrup is formed.

For the blackberry coulis – this adds a bit of tart flavour to the dish – simply place the blackberries in a small pan with 100ml water and the icing sugar. Simmer until reduced by half, then purée in a blender or food processor. Pass the mixture through a fine sieve to remove the seeds... voilà!

Preheat the oven to 150°C/gas mark 2.

For the hazelnut crumb, place the hazelnuts on a baking tray and toast for around 20 minutes or until golden brown. Leave to cool and then crush.

Serve the pears warm and the coulis and syrup at room temperature. To plate up, I do a nice swipe of coulis on the plate, then stand up a pear next to a slice of the parfait. To finish, sprinkle over the hazelnuts, and drizzle with a little mulled wine syrup...winter wonderland is here!

CROISSANT BREAD & BUTTER PUDDING WITH ROASTED PLUMS

We used to cook this in the chalet with day-old croissants and it's gorgeous! Serves 8

400ML MILK
400ML DOUBLE CREAM
1 VANILLA POD, SEEDS ONLY
150G CASTER SUGAR
6 MEDIUM EGGS
12 CROISSANTS, CUT IN HALF
    LENGTHWAYS
100G RAISINS

FOR THE ROASTED PLUMS
8 PLUMS, PITTED AND QUARTERED
50G DEMERARA SUGAR
2 STAR ANISE
SPLASH OF WATER

Heat the milk and cream in a saucepan until they come to the boil, then reduce the heat, add the vanilla seeds and sugar, and simmer for a few minutes. In the meantime, beat the eggs in a bowl, then slowly whisk them into the warm milk and cream, stirring continuously, to make a custard.

Lay half the croissant halves on roasting tin lined with baking parchment, sprinkle the raisins over the top, then add another layer of croissants.

Pour over the custard and allow to rest for 15 minutes whilst you preheat the oven to 160°C/gas mark 3. Place the roasting tin into a slightly larger roasting tin half-filled with boiling water. Carefully transfer to the oven and bake for 45 minutes, or until the custard has set.

For the roasted plums, cut them into quarters, discarding the stones, and roast with the demeraera sugar and cinnamon in an oven at 180°C/gas mark 4 for 20 minutes, or until soft. Serve the warm plums on the side.

CHOCOLATE TORTE WITH CRYSTALLIZED MINT

A dessert that doesn't even require any cooking!

FOR THE BASE
250G GINGER BISCUITS
1 TABLESPOON GOLDEN SYRUP
100G UNSALTED BUTTER, MELTED

FOR THE TORTE MIX
150G DARK CHOCOLATE, BROKEN
  INTO SMALL PIECES
100G MILK CHOCOLATE, BROKEN
  INTO SMALL PIECES
1 TEASPOON VANILLA EXTRACT
500ML DOUBLE CREAM

FOR THE MINT LEAVES
20 SMALL MINT LEAVES
2 EGG WHITES, BEATEN
2 TABLESPOONS ICING SUGAR
100G GRANULATED SUGAR

Line a 22cm springform cake tin with greaseproof paper.

To make the base, crush the biscuits by placing them in a freezer bag and giving them a few whacks on the work surface. Release some aggression! Combine the crumbs, golden syrup and butter, and press the biscuit mix into the prepared tin to form the base.

Melt both types of chocolate in a heatproof bowl au bain-marie, then remove from the heat and stir in the vanilla. In a separate, larger bowl, whip the cream until it just holds peaks, then fold the chocolate into the cream. Pour the mixture into the cake tin and leave to set in the fridge for at least 3 hours.

To make the crystallized mint leaves, preheat the oven to 60–70°C. Thoroughly mix the egg whites with the icing sugar. Rub each mint leaf gently with the mixture, then sprinkle the granulated sugar over the leaves. Place the coated leaves on a baking tray and bake for 1 hour (but keep checking after 30 minutes) until they are crispy and dry. Sprinkle them round the plate as a lovely garnish.

JIM'S ETON MESS

This classic is so easy to do – it's all in the meringues. Perfect on a summer's day, it was a featured dessert at my very first pop-up in my front room a few years ago. At weddings, we present it as a Very Eton Messy, and build huge towers of meringue, coulis, fruit, cream and jellies. We once did it for 500 people at a barbecue – it got VERY messy! The addition of basil may seem strange, but the combination of aromatic basil and sweet berries works really well together. Serves 6

FOR THE MERINGUE
4 EGG WHITES
300G CASTER SUGAR

FOR THE JELLY
500ML ELDERFLOWER CORDIAL
8 GELATINE LEAVES
2 BASIL LEAVES, FINELY
   CHOPPED

FOR THE COULIS
200G FROZEN RASPBERRIES
75G ICING SUGAR

FOR THE STRAWBERRY CREAM
100G FROZEN STRAWBERRIES
50G ICING SUGAR
200ML DOUBLE CREAM, WHIPPED
FRESH STRAWBERRIES, TO
   DECORATE

There are three rules to making good meringues:
1 Use a scrupulously clean bowl – preferably metal.
2 The egg whites need to be at room temperature.
3 Use good eggs!

So, time to get cracking... preheat the oven to 110°C/gas mark ¼. Line a large baking tray with baking parchment.

Whisk the egg whites to stiff peaks, then add the sugar very slowly, continuing to whisk. This'll keep them nice and stiff, so they hold their shape in the oven. Spread into a layer on the prepared baking tray – no fuss just get it on!

Cook in the oven for 1½ hours, then turn off the oven and leave them inside for as long as possible without opening the door, so they can dry out and become crunchy.

To make the jelly, heat the elderflower cordial in a small pan with 500ml water. Meanwhile, soak the gelatine leaves in cold water. When the elderflower liquid comes to the boil, take off the heat and stir in the drained gelatine. Pour into a plastic container and transfer to the fridge to set. Once the mixture has begun to set, stir in the basil.

For the coulis, heat the raspberries in a pan with 100ml water and the icing sugar, and allow to simmer for 15 minutes. Then purée in a blender or food processor, pass the mixture through a fine sieve to remove the seeds then chill. Done.

For the strawberry cream, make a strawberry coulis, as above. Lightly fold the coulis into the whipped cream to give a marbled effect.

When it comes to plating up, cut the jelly into cubes, and get creative... The plate's your canvas! Assemble with one meringue at the bottom topped with a huge dollop of strawberry cream, followed by another meringue, more cream, and coulis drizzled over the top. Finely chop the eldeflower jelly and spread chunks around the outside.

APPLE GRATIN, NUT & OAT CRUMB, MINI TOFFEE APPLE, MARSHMALLOW & BLACKBERRY COULIS

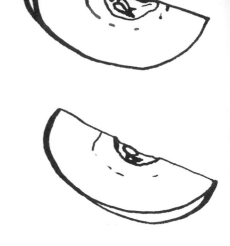

This is my take on apple crumble. Serves 4 – with plenty left over!

FOR THE APPLE GRATIN
2KG PINK LADY APPLES, PEELED, CORED AND CUT INTO 1CM THICK SLICES
100G DEMERARA SUGAR
3 TABLESPOONS GROUND CINNAMON
50G BUTTER, CUT INTO THIN SLICES

FOR THE BLACKBERRY COULIS
200G BLACKBERRIES
50G ICING SUGAR

FOR THE MINI TOFFEE APPLES
100G CASTER SUGAR
4 BALLS OF PINK LADY APPLES (USE A MELON BALLER)

FOR THE CRUMBLE TOPPING
50G CRUSHED HAZELNUTS
50G OATS
100G PLAIN FLOUR
50G DEMERARA SUGAR
75G UNSALTED BUTTER, CUBED

FOR THE MARSHMALLOW GARNISH
100G MARSHMALLOWS
20ML COLD WATER

To make the apple gratin, preheat the oven to 160°C/gas mark 3. Line a terrine dish with baking parchment and layer the apple slices in between sprinklings of the sugar, cinnamon and butter. Cover the top with more baking parchment and roast for about 45 minutes.

In the meantime, make the blackberry coulis. Place the blackberries and icing sugar, along with 100ml cold water, into a small saucepan. Simmer over a medium heat for about 15 minutes until the liquid reduces by half. Blitz, using a stick blender, and then pass the contents through a sieve to remove the pips. Allow to cool.

For the apples, heat the sugar in a saucepan until it reaches 62°C (use a kitchen thermometer), and then impale the balls of apple onto lollipop sticks and dip them into the melted sugar, ensuring they are completely coated in the caramel. Insert the sticks into a Styrofoam block to set.

To make the crumble topping, increase the oven temperature to 200°C/gas mark 6. Place all the ingredients into a bowl and rub in the butter using your fingertips until fully combined. Line a baking tray with greaseproof paper and spread the crumble mix over the tray. Bake for 15 minutes, until golden brown, then remove from the oven and crumble up the mixture.

For the marshmallow garnish, melt the marshmallows in a saucepan with the water. When melted, spread on a plate and sit the toffee apples on top alongside the remaining ingredients, and there you have my 'crumble!'.

RICE PUDDING

A lovely, rich rice pudding, with a nice gooseberry compote ... boom! Serves 6

150G ARBORIO RICE
2 LITRES WHOLE MILK
130G CASTER SUGAR
2 TABLESPOONS VANILLA ESSENCE

FOR THE COMPOTE
400G GOOSEBERRIES
75G CASTER SUGAR
JUICE AND ZEST OF 1 ORANGE.
1 STAR ANISE

Preheat the oven to 150°C/gas mark 2.

Thoroughly wash the rice in a colander until the water runs clear. This removes all of the starchiness that can make the pudding overly thick.

Place all of the ingredients in a large saucepan and bring to the boil, then reduce to a simmer. Cook for about 30 minutes, stirring occasionally to prevent the rice from sticking to the bottom.

Meanwhile, make the compote. Place all of the ingredients in a saucepan and bring to the boil. Reduce to a simmer and cook over a medium heat for about 25 minutes. Remove from the heat and allow to cool. You should have a lovely gooseberry delight to go with the rice pudding!

Once the rice has cooked, spoon the mixture into individual ramekins and bake in the oven for 25 minutes. You can serve this either cold (which I prefer), or straight from the oven. Place a little gooseberry compote on top and you're done.

JIMMY'S ICE CREAM FACTORY

This is a hugely popular dish that's been the staple dessert for many of my restaurants. The idea came from childhood memories of going to a well-known pizza chain and having DIY ice cream. In my version, we make some fantastic toppings and a delicious, quick and easy raspberry sorbet as a variation on ice cream. You can either make the toppings, or buy them, and the same goes with the ice cream, but it's a great way to get everyone talking and having fun round the dinner table. I like to place all the toppings in jam jars for an authentic sweet-shop feel! Serves 8

FOR THE SORBET
250G CASTER SUGAR
500G FROZEN RASPBERRIES
½ LIME
3 TABLESPOONS RASPBERRY
    LIQUEUR (CHAMBORD)

FOR THE COOKIES
125G BUTTER, SOFTENED
100G BROWN SUGAR
125G CASTER SUGAR
1 TEASPOON VANILLA EXTRACT
1 EGG
250G SELF-RAISING FLOUR
½ TEASPOON SALT
50G MILK CHOCOLATE CHIPS
50G WHITE CHOCOLATE CHIPS

FOR THE TOPPINGS
MINI MARSHMALLOWS
HUNDREDS AND THOUSANDS
CRUSHED MERINGUES (SEE ETON
    MESS, PAGE 112)
BROWNIE CHUNKS (SEE BROWNIES,
    PAGE 105)
SHORTBREAD (SEE TRIFLE,
    PAGE 118)
RASPBERRY COULIS (SEE ETON
    MESS, PAGE 112)
FRESH FRUIT JELLY (PAGE 112)
COOKIE CHUNKS (SEE ABOVE)

First make the sorbet. Place 500ml water and the sugar in a medium pan, and bring to the boil. Stir for around 3 minutes, until the sugar has dissolved, and then allow to cool.

Place the raspberries in a pan with a squeeze of lime. Cook until soft, then purée in a blender or food processor and pass the mixture through a fine sieve to remove the seeds. Pour the raspberry purée and liqueur into the sugar syrup, and stir thoroughly before transferring to an ice-cream maker. Churn according to the instructions, transfer to an airtight lidded container and freeze for at least 12 hours or until solid.

Alternatively, if you don't have an ice-cream maker, pour the mixture into an airtight lidded container and transfer to the freezer. Remove from the freezer every hour or so, and stir well to crush the ice crystals with the back of a fork. This will help to create a smoother sorbet rather than an ice block – the best results are with an ice-cream maker, but sometimes you have to make good with what you have!

Preheat the oven to 180°C/gas mark 4. Line a baking tray with baking parchment.

For the cookies, cream the butter and sugars together in a medium bowl until light and fluffy. Stir in the vanilla and the egg. Sift in the flour and salt, then add the chocolate chips. Stir well to combine. Place about 6 chestnut-sized dollops on the baking tray, spaced well apart. Bake in the oven for 8 minutes. They should still be soft, and gooey! Cool on a wire rack. These also go down a storm served with the Boozy Chocolate Shake (page 128).

Crumble all of the toppings into jam jars, or bowls if you don't have them, so you can try to recreate that ultimate sundae, sweet-shop feel!

21ST-CENTURY TRIFLE

A twist on the traditional trifle we have all grown to love. Many a family dinner has been finished with a huge spoonful of Mama Garcia's infamous trifle! Here, I've taken the components for an Orange and Berry Trifle and presented them in a contemporary way, but feel free to mix up the fruits to tickle your fancy! Serves 6

FOR THE ORANGE AND COINTREAU JELLY
200ML FRESH ORANGE JUICE
2 TABLESPOONS COINTREAU
4 GELATINE LEAVES

FOR THE CLEMENTINE GENOISE SPONGE
6 MEDIUM EGGS
200G CASTER SUGAR
ZEST OF 2 CLEMENTINES
50G BUTTER, MELTED
200G PLAIN FLOUR

FOR THE GINGER SHORTBREAD
125G BUTTER
70G CASTER SUGAR
200G PLAIN FLOUR, PLUS EXTRA
   FOR DUSTING
2 TABLESPOONS GROUND GINGER

FOR THE CRÈME ANGLAISE
200ML SEMI-SKIMMED MILK
200ML DOUBLE CREAM
1 VANILLA POD, SPLIT
   LENGTHWAYS
5 MEDIUM EGG YOLKS
150G CASTER SUGAR
CRÈME FRAÎCHE AND FRESH
   BERRIES, TO SERVE

Heat the orange juice and Cointreau in a small pan. Meanwhile, soak the gelatine leaves in cold water.

Once the juice mix is almost up to the boil, take off the heat and add the drained gelatine leaves, stir, and then transfer to a 12 x 15cm plastic container. Allow to set in the fridge for at least 10 hours.

Preheat the oven to 180°/gas mark 4. Line a 24 x 18cm baking tray with baking parchment.

To make the sponge, whisk the eggs and sugar in a medium bowl, using an electric hand whisk, until thick and pale. Carefully fold in the zest, melted butter and flour, to keep the air in – this helps the sponge rise.

Pour the mixture into the prepared tray and bake for about 20 minutes or until the sponge has risen. Remove from the oven, but leave the oven on. Leave in the tray to cool for 10 minutes and then transfer to a wire rack to cool completely.

Line a second baking tray with baking parchment.

For the ginger shortbread, cream the butter and sugar together in a medium bowl, until light and fluffy. Stir in the flour and ginger, to form a smooth dough. Roll out on a floured work surface to a thickness of 5mm and place on the lined tray. Bake for around 15 minutes. Remove from the oven and leave on the tray to cool for 10 minutes before transfering to a wire rack to cool completely.

Whilst all these bits and bobs are going in the oven, we can get on with a crème anglaise on the hob!

For the crème anglaise (this is basically a cold, silky custard!), heat the milk, cream and vanilla pod in a small pan over a medium heat. Once it is simmering, reduce to a low heat.

In a medium bowl whisk the egg yolks and sugar, before slowly adding them to the pan, stirring constantly until the mix begins to coat the back of a spoon. Once cooked, to avoid it cooking further and splitting, transfer the crème into a heatproof jug and place it in a bowl of iced water to cool. Once cooled to room temperature, pour it into shot glasses.

To serve, place a shot glass of crème anglaise onto each plate. Cut the sponge into rectangles and the jelly into ice-cube-size blocks and arrange on the plate, the jelly stacked on top of the sponge. Crush the shortbread into large crumbs and scatter round the plate, then to finish, add fresh berries and pipe some crème fraîche!

COCKTAILS

ULTIMATE MULLED WINE

I couldn't have had a pop-up called The Lodge and serve hot cocktails without mastering the ultimate mulled wine, so here it is! I used to serve this in 1-litre flasks on the table for everyone to dive in and share. Makes about 700ml.

500ML RED WINE
100ML ORANGE JUICE
80ML CHERRY BRANDY
80ML PISCO PORTÓN RUM
2 CINNAMON STICKS
2 STAR ANISE
1 BAY LEAF
1 CLOVE
50G BROWN SUGAR
GENEROUS GRATING OF NUTMEG
   (APPROX 1 TEASPOON)
ZEST OF ½ ORANGE
ORANGE SLICES AND CINNAMON
   STICKS, TO DECORATE

Place all the ingredients into a large saucepan over a low heat for about 40 minutes. Do not allow the liquid to come to the boil; it should get to a point where it's just too hot to dip your finger in. We don't want to burn away all that alcohol!

Garnish each glass with a slice of orange and a cinnamon stick.

ROYAL MULLED CIDER

This always goes down a storm and is a great alternative to the more usual mulled wine. Serves 6

660ML PEAR CIDER
1 CINNAMON STICK
4 CARDAMOM PODS
5CM PIECE OF FRESH ROOT GINGER,
   PEELED AND CHOPPED
1 TEASPOON GROUND NUTMEG
3 STAR ANISE, PLUS EXTRA
   TO SERVE
240ML THE KING'S GINGER LIQUEUR
1 PEAR, SLICED INTO 6
1 ORANGE, SLICED

Heat all the ingredients in a pan to a simmer, but do not boil, as you don't want to reduce the alcohol.

Remove from the heat and allow all the flavours to infuse for at least 1 hour before serving.

Reheat and garnish with a pear slice over the edge of the glass and on orange slice with a star anise in the middle.

HOT BUTTERED RUM

A signature cocktail from the pop-up
I did at The Lodge. Needless to say, it
was a hit! Serves 1

100ML PINEAPPLE JUICE
1 CINNAMON STICK
20G UNSALTED BUTTER
1 TABLESPOON DEMERARA SUGAR
50ML ELEMENTS 8 SPICED RUM
   OR ANY SPICED DARK RUM
2 PINEAPPLE CHUNKS AND 1 MINI
   MERINGUE, TO DECORATE

Heat all the ingredients except the rum in a small
saucepan; allow the cinnamon stick to infuse and
the butter to melt. Then simply add the rum – no
need to burn off all the good alcohol!

Pour into heatproof glasses, garnish with the
pineapple chunks and mini meringue and enjoy!

BACON, BOURBON & MAPLE

This drink works really well and is served over ice, or with a dash of water if it's too strong for your taste. Makes 1 litre

100G LARDONS OR BACON FAT
1 LITRE BOTTLE OF BOURBON
   (JACK DANIEL'S IS FINE)
ICE CUBES
1 TEASPOON MAPLE SYRUP
JUICE OF ¼ LEMON
PORK SCRATCHINGS (SEE PORK
   AND APPLES ON PAGE 92 FOR
   THE CRACKLING), TO SERVE

Melt the lardons in the microwave and pour out a small amount of bourbon from the bottle, before pouring the melted fat into the bottle. Screw the cap back on and give it a good shake. Leave to infuse for 1 week.

After a week, strain the bourbon through a fine wire mesh to leave behind the lardons, then transfer the bourbon back into the bottle, and it's ready to use!

In a rocks glass with lots of ice, pour 50ml infused bourbon and stir in the maple syrup and lemon juice. Serve with some pork scratchings on the side.

GIN GARDEN

A tasty summer cocktail packed with all my favourite flavours. Serves 1

50ML GIN
10ML ELDERFLOWER CORDIAL
100ML APPLE JUICE
3 LIME WEDGES
5 SLICES OF CUCUMBER
ICE CUBES
50ML TONIC WATER

Place the gin, cordial and apple juice in a Boston shaker along with the lime wedges and muddled cucumber (see page 127). Shake well.

Pour into a highball glass over ice and top up with the tonic. There you have it – a taste of British summer!

LONDON LIVENER

I created this cocktail to mark the launch of the TV channel London Live where I made my very first TV appearance. I wanted a something that would liven up the party by playing on the phrase 'apples and pears' and then added some Prosecco for good measure! Serves 1

40ML VODKA
20ML PEAR LIQUEUR
1 TABLESPOON PEAR PURÉE
50ML PROSECCO
50ML APPLE JUICE
APPLE AND PEAR SLICES,
   TO DECORATE

Combine all the ingredients in a Boston cocktail shaker, if possible. These are your regular shakers and are available in most big supermarkets now! Otherwise, mix everything together in a jug. Pour into large champagne flutes and top up with Prosecco. Decorate with apple and pear slices.

BLUEBERRY & BASIL MOJITO(S)

Whilst I was at uni in Newcastle I worked in a cocktail bar. Needless to say, mojitos were generally the order of the day. This is a quirky twist on the original classic – I've swapped white rum for dark and added a generous splash of pomegranate and blueberry juice instead of lime juice; basil leaves take the place of fresh mint but lime wedges, to garnish, act as a nod to the traditional recipe. Serves 1

1 TABLESPOON SOFT BROWN SUGAR
2 TABLESPOONS BLUEBERRIES, PLUS
  EXTRA TO DECORATE
9 BASIL LEAVES, PLUS EXTRA
  TO DECORATE
3 LIME WEDGES, PLUS EXTRA
  TO DECORATE
6 TABLESPOONS CRUSHED ICE
50ML DARK RUM
50ML POMEGRANATE AND BLUEBERRY
  JUICE
A SPLASH OF SODA WATER

Place the brown sugar, blueberries, basil leaves and lime wedges in a jug and muddle (see tip) until the blueberries are crushed. Add the ice, then pour in the rum and juice. Give it a stir with a cocktail spoon or long-handled teaspoon until fully mixed. Pour into a 10oz glass and top up with soda, decorate with a wedge of lime, a few blueberries and a sprig of basil.

TIP

To muddle means to press or mash ingredients. A muddler is similar to a long-handled pestle with a narrow flat end (used to stir and mix ingredients). A pestle or wooden spoon can be used instead of a muddler.

BOOZY CHOCOLATE SHAKE

A chocolate lover's dream... no need to say any more! Serves 1

25ML BAILEYS ORIGINAL IRISH
   CREAM
25ML COINTREAU
15ML CHOCOLATE LIQUEUR, SUCH
   AS MOZART DARK
50ML WHOLE MILK
50ML SINGLE CREAM
1 TABLESPOON MELTED MILK
   CHOCOLATE
6 TABLESPOONS CRUSHED ICE
ORANGE SLICES, TO GARNISH

Place all the ingredients in a cocktail shaker or jug and combine until fully mixed. I like to serve this in old-fashioned milk bottles, but otherwise pour into 10oz glasses and decorate with orange slices.

AFTER PARTY

BRUNCH

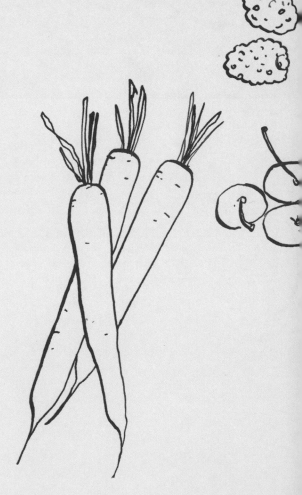

BERRY & MANGO SMOOTHIE

A delicious start to the day, this smoothie is packed with vitamins and a great way to use up that slightly overripe fruit. Serves 1

1 VERY RIPE BANANA, CHOPPED
100G FROZEN RASPBERRIES
100G FRESH MANGO, CHOPPED
2 TABLESPOONS NATURAL YOGURT
50ML MANGO PULP
50ML APPLE JUICE

Place all the ingredients into a food processor and whizz until combined. Serve in a tall pint glass and get ready to rumble!

CELERY, APPLE, CARROT & GINGER DETOX

This is an excellent smoothie for those feeling a little delicate from the night before. Ideally, you need a juicer, or you can buy the fruit/vegetable juices from the supermarket. I used to make this in a private chalet every morning – 3 litres of the stuff! Serves 1

1 APPLE (OR 70ML APPLE JUICE)
1 CARROT (OR 70ML CARROT JUICE)
1 LARGE CELERY STICK
1 THUMB-SIZED PIECE OF GINGER, PEELED
CELERY STICK AND CARROT RIBBON, TO SERVE

Put all the ingredients into a food processor (or juicer if using the whole fruit/vegetable). Whizz until combined and serve with a stick of celery and a carrot ribbon in the glass.

BEEFY BLOODY MARY

Everyone needs a good hangover cure in their bag of tricks, and a Bloody Mary is a staple for most people. Many a time have I called upon this beauty to get me out of the hard times the morning after the night before. Serves 1

3 TABLESPOONS CHILLED BEEF
  STOCK
125ML TOMATO JUICE
50ML VODKA
JUICE OF ½ LEMON
DASH OF CELERY SALT
3 DASHES WORCESTERSHIRE SAUCE
3 DASHES OF TABASCO SAUCE
FRESHLY GROUND BLACK PEPPER
5 ICE CUBES AND CRUSHED ICE,
  TO SERVE
CELERY STICKS AND LEMON
  SLICES, TO GARNISH

Place all the ingredients in a Boston cocktail shaker or a jug, season with freshly ground black pepper and add the ice cubes, give it a good old shake or a stir and pour into a glass filled with crushed ice. Garnish with celery and lemon.

POSH HANGOVER EGGS ROYALE

This is my girlfriend's favourite, and is pretty easy to make if you get your hollandaise right. Serves 1

1 SLICE OF BRIOCHE
50G SMOKED SALMON
2 POACHED EGGS
SMALL HANDFUL OF CHIVES,
  CHOPPED, TO GARNISH

FOR THE HOLLANDAISE
2 MEDIUM EGG YOLKS, BEATEN
SPLASH OF ICE-COLD WATER
1 TEASPOON TARRAGON VINEGAR
125G MELTED BUTTER
SQUEEZE OF LEMON
½ TEASPOON PAPRIKA
SALT AND FRESHLY GROUND
  BLACK PEPPER

To make the hollandaise sauce, place the egg yolks, water and vinegar in a small heatproof bowl and sit over a small pan of simmering water. Whisk over a low heat for about 5 minutes, until the mixture becomes pale and thick.

Remove the bowl from the heat and slowly add the melted butter, whisking continuously. Add a squeeze of lemon juice, the paprika and a touch of seasoning.

Toast the brioche, sit the salmon and poached eggs on top, spoon over the hollandaise and garnish with the chopped chives.

POACHED EGG, ASPARAGUS & CHAMPIGNONS DE PARIS

A quick and tasty brunch to enjoy on a lazy Sunday perhaps. Serves 2

4 EGGS
SPLASH OF WHITE WINE VINEGAR,
  FOR POACHING
DRIZZLE OF OLIVE OIL
8 ASPARAGUS SPEARS
100G WHITE MUSHROOMS, VERY
  THINLY SLICED
JUICE OF ½ LEMON
SALT AND FRESHLY GROUND
  BLACK PEPPER
2 SLICES OF TOAST, TO SERVE

To poach the perfect egg, see recipe on page 140.

Heat a little oil in a griddle pan and cook the asparagus spears over a high heat for 3 minutes on each side. Season with salt and black pepper.

Lay the mushroom slices on a baking tray, drizzle with a little oil, the lemon juice and seasoning. Set aside, covered with foil.

To serve, place all the ingredients on top of a slice of toast and get eating in front of some daytime TV!

HUEVOS RANCHEROS

So you had some friends round last night, it was a big one, and there are bodies strewn all over the floor when you wake up at 11am (it was a late one, too!). There's only one smell wafting through the air that can get most grown men out of their slumber. Huevos rancheros – fried eggs and refried beans with Cajun spices. This is so easy and has a South American slapdash, flavoursome feel to it. Serves 4

2 TABLESPOONS OLIVE OIL
1 RED PEPPER, DESEEDED AND
   FINELY CHOPPED
1 RED ONION, SLICED
2 GARLIC CLOVES, FINELY
   CHOPPED
½ RED CHILLI, DESEEDED AND
   FINELY CHOPPED
400G CAN KIDNEY BEANS,
   DRAINED AND RINSED
½ X 400G CAN BORLOTTI BEANS,
   DRAINED AND RINSED
200ML PASSATA
2 TEASPOONS CAJUN SEASONING
2 TEASPOONS PAPRIKA
SALT AND FRESHLY GROUND
   BLACK PEPPER
4 MEDIUM EGGS
1 AVOCADO, PITTED AND DICED
SMALL BUNCH OF CORIANDER,
   TO GARNISH
FRENCH BREAD TOAST, TO SERVE

Heat 20ml of the oil in a medium frying pan over a medium heat and cook the pepper for 5 minutes, and then add the onion, garlic and chilli and cook for another 5 minutes or until softened. Add the kidney beans and borlotti beans to the pan, and fry until they begin to soften, about 6 minutes.

Add the passata, a splash of water and the spices, and season. Allow the flavours to come together and cook to reduce the sauce to a thick consistency.

Heat the remaining oil in a large frying pan over a medium heat and fry the eggs for about 3 minutes, basting them with the oil to speed up the process.

Place the bean mix on 4 plates, followed by an egg and a spoonful of diced avocado plus some torn up coriander!

Serve with some French bread toast and wave goodbye to that hangover!

POACHED EGGS WITH CREAMED WILD MUSHROOMS ON TOAST

This has got to be my ultimate breakfast – simple, tasty, and quick to do on a hangover! Serves 1

SPLASH OF WHITE WINE VINEGAR
2 MEDIUM EGGS
LARGE KNOB OF BUTTER
1 GARLIC CLOVE, FINELY
    CHOPPED
100G WILD MUSHROOMS, PICKED,
    WASHED AND CHOPPED
3 TABLESPOONS DOUBLE CREAM
SMALL BUNCH OF CURLY LEAF
    PARSLEY, FINELY CHOPPED
SALT AND FRESHLY GROUND
    BLACK PEPPER
SOURDOUGH TOAST, TO SERVE

To make the perfect poached eggs isn't difficult, all you need is a small pan of salted water with a splash of white wine vinegar. Bring the water up to a simmer, and then just before dropping in the eggs, whisk the water, to create a 'whirlpool' motion. Carefully crack the eggs in, in a single motion and cook for 3 minutes. Remove with a slotted spoon and you should have the perfect poached eggs!

Whilst the eggs are poaching, melt the butter in a medium frying pan over a medium heat and fry the garlic and mushrooms for 5 minutes until soft.

Add the cream and the parsley. Allow the cream to heat through, and season.

Serve on some lovely sourdough toast. Say goodbye to that hangover!

TORTILLA À LA PAPA G

My dad is a super cool Spaniard... passionate about food and wine and with terrible jokes to boot! He's the person who inspired me to cook and he has a repertoire of home favourites only bettered by my late grandma. I've had many a Spanish omelette in my time, and for this one I've added chargrilled vegetables, just to mix it up a little. Easy, and a lovely lunchtime alternative to a sandwich. Serves 6

150ML OLIVE OIL
2KG RED POTATOES, CUT INTO
   1CM CUBES
1KG SWEET POTATOES, CUT INTO
   1CM CUBES
1 RED PEPPER, DESEEDED AND
   FINELY CHOPPED
1 COURGETTE, FINELY CHOPPED
1 ONION, FINELY DICED
3 GARLIC CLOVES, FINELY
   CHOPPED
7 MEDIUM EGGS, BEATEN
2 TABLESPOONS DRIED OREGANO
1 TABLESPOON FRESH THYME
   LEAVES
1 TABLESPOON CHOPPED
   FRESH BASIL
SALT AND FRESHLY GROUND
   BLACK PEPPER

Preheat the oven to 180°C/gas mark 4.

Heat 30ml of the olive oil in a medium ovenproof frying pan and sauté the red potatoes in batches, for 10 minutes or until almost cooked through, then transfer to a plate lined with kitchen paper to drain off any excess oil.

In the same pan, fry the sweet potato chunks in 30ml oil until cooked through, for 8 minutes, then transfer to a plate lined with kitchen paper. Do the same with the pepper and courgette, cooking in 30ml oil for around 6 minutes on a medium heat. Set these to one side before adding the onion and garlic and 30ml oil to the pan. Cook for 6 minutes or until softened.

Add the remaining oil to the frying pan, then return all the sautéed veg to the pan, with the beaten eggs, oregano, thyme, basil and seasoning. Fry over a low heat for 7 minutes. Then transfer to the oven for around 10 minutes, or until cooked through.

Transfer the tortilla to a wire cooling rack, and then serve either hot or cold, in a sandwich, with salad, or as tapas.

HOMEMADE GRANOLA & BERRY COMPOTE

I love granola, whether it's for breakfast or a snack, and it's such an easy thing to make. Serves 6

FOR THE GRANOLA
50G FLAKED ALMONDS
50G MACADAMIA NUTS
50G HAZELNUTS
100G OATS
50G RAISINS
50G DRIED APRICOTS, FINELY DICED
50G DRIED CRANBERRIES, FINELY DICED
3 MEDIUM EGG WHITES, BEATEN
50G GRANULATED SUGAR
GREEK YOGURT, TO SERVE

FOR THE COMPOTE
300G FROZEN BERRIES
2 TABLESPOONS ICING SUGAR

Preheat the oven to 140°C/gas mark 1½.

Start by making the granola. Put all the ingredients into a mixing bowl and mix well with your hands. Transfer to a roasting tin and bake for about 30 minutes, or until golden and in clusters. Easy peasy!

For the compote, put the berries and icing sugar into a small saucepan along with 100ml cold water and bring to the boil, then reduce the heat and simmer for 15 minutes, until the liquid has reduced by two-thirds. Set aside and leave to cool before serving on top of the granola with a dollop of Greek yogurt. Breakfast of champions!

ALL-AMERICAN PANCAKES

We do these beauties every Tuesday in our chalet, and the crowd always goes wild for them… they're so quick and tasty, and great stodge for the morning after the night before! Makes enough for 12 thick pancakes (2 each)

12 RASHERS STREAKY BACON
220G PLAIN FLOUR, SIFTED
300ML SEMI-SKIMMED MILK
2 MEDIUM EGGS
1½ TEASPOONS BAKING POWDER
PINCH OF SALT
40G BUTTER, MELTED, PLUS
  EXTRA FOR FRYING
3 BANANAS, SLICED
  MAPLE SYRUP, TO SERVE

Preheat the oven to 180°C/gas mark 4.

Place the bacon on a non-stick baking tray and cook in the oven for 15–20 minutes, until nice and crispy. Whilst the bacon's in the oven, crack on with the pancakes.

Place the flour, milk, eggs, baking powder, salt and melted butter in a food processor and whizz until fully combined.

Heat a large heavy-based frying pan over a medium heat and add a knob of butter. Once the butter has melted, add a small ladleful of the pancake batter mixture to the pan. When small pockets of air form on the surface, give it a flip, and cook both sides until lightly golden. Repeat with the remaining batter to make 12 pancakes in total.

To serve, place 2 pancakes, 2 rashers of bacon and a few banana slices on each plate, and drench with lashings of good old maple syrup!

WINNER!

MOULES À LA PAPA G

On a Sunday afternoon in my house growing up we used to love cooking seafood and this was always a winner. This is a really great rustic dish – lovely cooked mussels in one pot, and then a big bowl of sauce with which to scoop up the mussels. Best to have plenty of napkins for this one! Serves 6

1 ONION, DICED
2 GARLIC CLOVES, CRUSHED
1 SMALL RED CHILLI, DESEEDED
   AND FINELY CHOPPED
20ML OLIVE OIL
175ML DRY WHITE WINE
2 BAY LEAVES
100ML FISH STOCK
800G FRESH TOMATOES (SLIGHTLY
   OVER-RIPE IF POSSIBLE),
FINELY CHOPPED
200G PITTED GREEN OLIVES
2KG LIVE MUSSELS, SCRUBBED
   AND BEARDS REMOVED (DISCARD
   ANY THAT STAY OPEN WHEN
   SHARPLY TAPPED)
BUNCH OF FRESH CORIANDER,
   FINELY CHOPPED
BUNCH OF FRESH CURLY LEAF
   PARSLEY, FINELY CHOPPED
FRESH BREAD, TO SERVE

In a medium pan, fry the onion, garlic and chilli in the olive oil over a medium heat until softened, and then add the wine, bay leaves, fish stock, tomatoes and olives (to give it a little tang – they taste delicious in this sauce) and allow to reduce.

Put the mussels in a large pan with a splash of fish stock, place on a medium heat and stir continuously for around 5 minutes. The mussels should begin to open, meaning they're cooked. Remove the mussels using a slotted spoon (reserving the cooking liquid) and set aside. Discard any unopened mussels (as these will give you a terrible tummy!).

Pour the mussel cooking liquid into the pan of sauce. Reduce for a further 12 minutes, add the coriander and parsley and reduce for 3 more minutes before serving everything together with chunks of fresh bread and digging in!

JIM'S INSALATA CAPRESE

This is such a great classic dish that our adaptation of it doesn't need much tweaking. We've just added anchovies and basil croutons. Serves 4

1 BUFFALO MOZZARELLA, SLICED
200G HERITAGE TOMATOES, SLICED
8 ANCHOVY FILLETS
1 CELERY STICK, FINELY CHOPPED
100G SEMI-DRIED TOMATOES (SEE
   PAGE 156)
50G ROCKET
¼ RED ONION, THINLY SLICED
GRINDING OF ROCK SALT

FOR THE DRESSING
25ML BASIL OIL
15ML BALSAMIC VINEGAR

FOR THE CROUTONS
5 SLICES OF DAY-OLD CRUSTY
   BREAD, CUT INTO CHUNKS
15ML BASIL OIL

Start by making the croutons. Preheat the oven to 150°C/gas mark 2. Place the chunks of bread onto a roasting tin, drizzle with 15ml of the basil oil, and bake for about 25 minutes, until crispy and hard!

To make the dressing, mix the basil oil and balsamic vinegar together.

To serve up, layer all the ingredients onto a serving dish and then drizzle over the dressing and season with rock salt.

THE ULTIMATE CHICKEN SANDWICH

ULTIMATE MINUTE STEAK SANDWICH

ULTIMATE MINUTE STEAK SANDWICH

STEAK! Most men's best friend! We're making a quick rustle that's perfect for a Saturday afternoon, or a treat when you've just got in from a long day at work. We're taking all the ingredients that make a great steak dinner (apart from the chips) and chucking them in the sarnie! Serves 1

150G SIRLOIN STEAK
6 CHERRY TOMATOES
SPLASH OF BALSAMIC VINEGAR
SPLASH OF OLIVE OIL
KNOB OF BUTTER
100G OYSTER MUSHROOMS,
    ROUGHLY CHOPPED
50G BLUE CHEESE, CRUMBLED
1 TEASPOON ENGLISH MUSTARD
ABOUT 10CM LONG PIECE OF
    FRESH CIABATTA
HANDFUL OF ROCKET
SALT AND FRESHLY GROUND
    BLACK PEPPER
MAYONNAISE, TO SERVE

Preheat the oven to 200°C/gas mark 6.

Place a nice piece of steak in between two 30cm pieces of clingfilm and hit with force, either with a mallet or the base of a saucepan.

Put the cherry tomatoes in a small ovenproof dish with a splash of balsamic and olive oil, and bake for 20 minutes.

Whilst the tommies are in the oven, heat a splash of oil and knob of butter in a small frying pan. Season the steak and fry it for around 2 minutes on each side over a high heat, taking care not to overcook the steak. Remove the steak and set aside on a warmed plate covered with foil to allow it to rest for 5 minutes.

Place the pan back on the hob, reduce the heat and add the mushrooms and cook them in the steak juices for 5 minutes. Toss the blue cheese into the pan with the mustard. Load the whole lot into a delicious ciabatta with a handful of rocket, the tomatoes, sliced steak (after it's had a rest!) and a wee smear of mayo – proper munchy food!

THE ULTIMATE CHICKEN SANDWICH

This is a great one for a cheeky indulgent snack! Leaves you licking your fingers. Serves 1

1 CHICKEN BREAST
50G PLAIN FLOUR
2 MEDIUM EGGS, BEATEN
100G PANKO BREADCRUMBS
100ML OLIVE OIL
KNOB OF BUTTER
2 SLICES PARMA HAM
6 SLICES CHORIZO
ABOUT 10CM LONG PIECE OF
    FRESH CIABATTA
100G MOZZARELLA, SLICED
EXTRA VIRGIN OLIVE OIL, FOR
    DRIZZLING
HANDFUL OF ROCKET
1 TOMATO, SLICED
SALT AND FRESHLY GROUND
    BLACK PEPPER

First up, butterfly the chicken. Make an incision with a knife down the side of the breast, running the knife horizontally through the breast but not all the way through. Lift the flap to create a butterflied breast, about half as thick but with a larger surface area!

Place the flour, eggs and breadcrumbs into 3 separate shallow dishes. Place the chicken in the flour, dip in the egg and then coat in the breadcrumbs. Dip in the egg and breadcrumbs again, for an extra crisp crust.

Preheat the oven to 200°C/gas mark 6.

Place the olive oil and butter in a frying pan, and once the oil is hot, fry the chicken over a medium heat for about 4 minutes on each side.

Place the Parma ham on a baking tray, and bake in the oven for 20 minutes, or until crispy. A couple of minutes before the end of the cooking time, add the chorizo to the tray to warm it up and allow the oil to begin to seep out.

Preheat the grill to high.

Slice the ciabatta lengthways down the middle, and add the slices of mozzarella and a generous glug of olive oil, before placing under the grill for 5 minutes, until the mozzarella begins to melt. Pile in the rest of the ingredients, season well, and don't forget to breathe between bites!!

ARANCINI & SALAD

Arancini – rice balls coated in breadcrumbs and fried – are an amazing way to use up leftover risotto. They're a really popular form of street food and really easy to do. See how to make a cracking risotto on page 170. Serves 2

FOR THE ARANCINI
200G LEFTOVER RISOTTO,
  CHILLED
50G PLAIN FLOUR
3 MEDIUM EGGS, LIGHTLY BEATEN
150G PANKO BREADCRUMBS
500ML VEGETABLE OIL FOR
  DEEP FRYING

FOR THE SALAD
100G CHERRY TOMATOES, HALVED
¼ CUCUMBER, DICED
100G ROCKET
50G GREEN OLIVES, PITTED
½ RED PEPPER, DESEEDED
  AND DICED
BALSAMIC VINEGAR, FOR
  DRIZZLING
EXTRA VIRGIN OLIVE OIL,
  FOR DRIZZLING
MALDON SEA SALT

To make the arancini balls, completely chill the risotto, before rolling into about 12 balls, about the size of golf balls.

Place the flour, eggs and breadcrumbs into 3 separate shallow dishes. Roll the balls in flour, dip in the egg and then roll in the breadcrumbs. Dip in the egg and breadcrumbs again, for an extra-crisp crust.

Heat the oil in a deep pan to 160°C (check with a kitchen thermometer or see page 22) and deep-fry the balls, in batches of 6 for around 5 minutes until golden. Remove, using a slotted spoon, and place onto a plate lined with kitchen paper, to absorb any excess oil. They will retain their heat for about 5 minutes, or place them in the bottom of a low oven at 120°C/gas mark ½.

Place the salad ingredients into a bowl, drizzle over the balsamic and olive oil, season with salt and serve with the hot rice balls. Enjoy!

COMFORT FOOD & SOUPS

CREAM OF PHEASANT, TRUFFLE & MUSTARD SOUP

I used to have a little business delivering soups to local cafés in London, and this was a favourite. 'Super-duper gourmet soup, brought to you by your local souper heroes!' Serves 6

1 WHOLE PHEASANT, LEGS AND
   BREAST SET ASIDE
500ML VEGETABLE OIL, PLUS
   EXTRA FOR FRYING

FOR THE SOUP
15ML TRUFFLE OIL, PLUS EXTRA
   FOR SERVING
100G BUTTER
2 ONIONS, CUT INTO CHUNKS
2 GARLIC CLOVES, CRUSHED
2 CELERY STICKS, FINELY
   CHOPPED
2 CARROTS, FINELY CHOPPED
1 LEEK
ZEST AND JUICE OF 1 ORANGE
150ML WHITE WINE
1 LITRE HOT CHICKEN STOCK
2 BAY LEAVES
4 SPRIGS OF THYME, LEAVES
   ONLY
100ML DOUBLE CREAM
FRESH TRUFFLE, FOR SHAVING

Preheat the oven to 130°C/gas mark 1.

First up, let's confit the pheasant legs. Place the legs into a small roasting tin and pour over the oil. Cover with foil and cook in the oven for about 3 hours, or until the meat flakes off the bone. Flake the meat into a bowl and set aside, ready to add to the soup.

After this time, increase the oven temperature to 200°C/gas mark 6. Heat a little oil in a heavy-based frying pan over a high heat and fry the pheasant breasts, skin-side down, for 5 minutes, then finish off in the oven for just 3 minutes. Remove from the oven and leave to rest for at least 5 minutes, then slice.

To make the soup, heat the truffle oil and butter in a large saucepan, then increase the heat and add the pheasant carcass, and cook for 5 minutes, before adding the onions, garlic, celery, carrots and leek. Fry for a further 5 minutes until soft. Once all the vegetables have softened, pour in the orange juice and wine and deglaze the pan. Reduce the liquor by half, then add the orange zest and juice, stock, bay leaves and thyme leaves. Bring to the boil, then cover and simmer for 2 hours.

Strain the liquor into a bowl and stir in the cream. Mix in the flaked leg meat.

Pour into bowls, place the slices of breast meat in the middle, and garnish with some freshly shaved truffle and a drizzle of truffle oil.

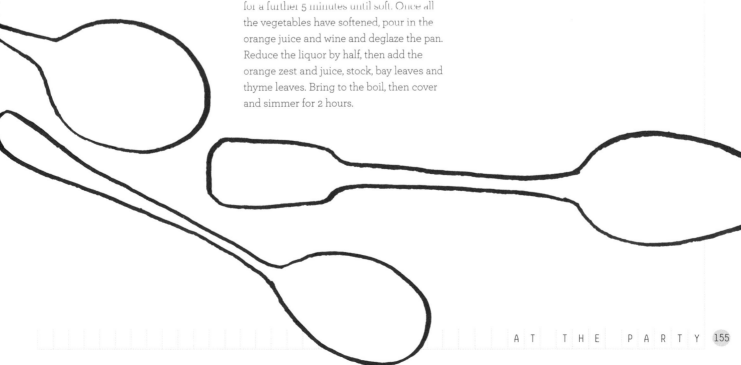

TOMATO, HONEY & CHILLI SOUP

This is a staple of mine; whenever I'm feeling a little tender, this little pick-me-up is exactly what's needed. I like to serve it with croutons and semi-dried tomatoes or a good old classic ham and cheese sandwich to dip in. Serves 4

2 TABLESPOONS OLIVE OIL
50G BUTTER
2 RED ONIONS, FINELY CHOPPED
2 GARLIC CLOVES, CRUSHED
1 CELERY STICK, CHOPPED
½ RED CHILLI, DESEEDED AND
  ROUGHLY CHOPPED
2 X 400G CANS CHOPPED
  TOMATOES
400ML VEGETABLE STOCK
1 TABLESPOON DRIED OREGANO
1 TABLESPOON DRIED THYME
2 TABLESPOONS CLEAR HONEY
SALT AND FRESHLY GROUND
  BLACK PEPPER

FOR THE SEMI-DRIED TOMATOES
6 CHERRY TOMATOES, HALVED
20G DRIED OREGANO

FOR THE CROUTONS
4 SLICES DAY-OLD BREAD, CUT
  INTO SQUARES

Heat the oil and butter in a medium pan over a medium heat and fry the onions, garlic, celery and chilli until softened.

Add the chopped tomatoes, stock, dried herbs and seasoning and allow to simmer for as long as possible – a minimum of 30 minutes should do it.

While the soup is bubbling away, if you fancy it, make some toppings for the soup. Preheat the oven to 150°C/gas mark 2. Place the tomatoes on a baking tray, sprinkle with the oregano and salt. Pop the bread squares on a separate tray. Transfer both trays to the oven and bake for 40 minutes.

Add the honey to the soup, and blend the soup with a hand-held electric blender until smooth.

Remove the tomatoes and bread from the oven and sprinkle over the soup, to serve. Job done!

CARROT, ORANGE & GINGER SOUP WITH CARROT CRISPS

When I first quit my job in the City to live the foodie dream full time, I started a soup company offering fresh home-made soups delivered daily to cafés, churches and businesses. This was one of the go-to favourites. Serves 6

FOR THE SOUP
50G BUTTER
2 TABLESPOONS OLIVE OIL
2 ONIONS, CHOPPED
1 CELERY STICK
7.5CM PIECE OF FRESH ROOT
  GINGER, PEELED AND GRATED
1KG CARROTS, CHOPPED
ZEST AND JUICE OF 2 ORANGES
1 LITRE VEGETABLE STOCK
CRÈME FRAÎCHE, TO GARNISH
SALT AND FRESHLY GROUND
  BLACK PEPPER

FOR THE CARROT CRISPS
500ML VEGETABLE OIL
2 CARROTS, CUT INTO RIBBONS
  WITH A RIBBON PEELER

Place the butter and olive oil in a large pan, add the onions, celery and ginger and fry over a medium heat until soft. Add the carrots and cook for another couple of minutes, then add the orange zest, juice and stock and bring to the boil before turning the heat right down and covering with a lid. Simmer until the carrots are fully cooked through, then blend the soup with a hand-held electric blender until smooth, adding more stock if it's a little thick.

Heat the oil in a frying pan to 160°C (check with a kitchen thermometer or see page 22), drop in the carrot ribbons and fry for 3–4 minutes (if the oil is hot enough they will immediately start to sizzle). Drain on kitchen paper and allow to cool and crisp.

Serve the soup in bowls with a small swirl of crème fraîche and the carrot crisps on top.

PEA & MINT VELOUTÉ

Velouté just means a thin and silky soup. I know what you're thinking. 'Soup's a cop-out', 'There's nothing fancy about soup' and 'My friends won't be blown away by bloody soup', but trust me, this variation looks – and tastes – really special. I once cooked it for a billionaire in his chalet in Courchevel, the kind of guy who spends €40million on a chalet, and then uses it for two weeks of the year.... So, this dish has a few components to it. First there's the soup, and then there's all the other garnishes that make it snazzy. Get the soup on the boil first, and allow it to simmer away, and in the meantime do all the faffy bits. If you can, it's best to let it cool overnight – everyone knows soup tastes better the next day! Serves 6

20ML VEGETABLE OIL
40G BUTTER
3 ONIONS, CHOPPED
2 GARLIC CLOVES, FINELY
    CHOPPED
2 CELERY STICKS, SLICED
2.5 LITRES VEGETABLE STOCK
250ML APPLE JUICE
1 BAY LEAF
2 TEASPOONS DRIED OREGANO
BUNCH OF THYME
1.5KG FROZEN PEAS
2 BUNCHES MINT
2 TABLESPOONS MAPLE SYRUP
SALT AND FRESHLY GROUND
    BLACK PEPPER

FOR THE GARNISHES
100ML OLIVE OIL
50G CHORIZO, CUT INTO 0.5CM
    CHUNKS
4 SLICES SERRANO HAM
ONE DAY-OLD BREAD
12 QUAILS' EGGS
50G PEA SHOOTS

Put the oil and butter (everything tastes better with a bit of butter!) in a large saucepan. Add the onions, garlic and celery and allow to sweat over a medium heat until cooked.

Add the veg stock, apple juice, bay leaf, oregano and thyme sprigs. Bring it to the boil, then cover with a lid and allow to simmer for a good hour at least, to let all the flavours come together.

Add the frozen peas, bring back to the boil and allow to simmer again until the peas are defrosted and cooked through. Add the mint and a splash of maple syrup, and give it a proper good blend with a hand-held electric blender until smooth. Once blended, allow it to cool in the pan, preferably overnight.

Next up, we're going to jazz it up, with lots of components to be put in the bowl, ready for the soup to be poured over.

For the chorizo oil, pour the olive oil into a small pan, to a depth of about 1cm, and add the chopped chunks of chorizo. Leave it on a low heat for about an hour until the oil has gone orange, and there you have it – chorizo oil.

To make the Serrano crisps, first preheat the oven to 150°C/gas mark 2 and line a baking tray with baking parchment. Next cut the slices of ham in half, diagonally, so you have big 'shards', and place them on the lined tray. Cover with another layer of baking parchment and another baking tray on top to flatten. Crisp the ham in the oven for about 40 minutes –1 hour.

Meanwhile, for the croutons, drizzle some of the chorizo oil on the bread, and cut the slices into uniform squares. Pop them onto a baking tray and bake them until nice and crispy, about 15 minutes.

Cook the quails' eggs in a medium pan of boiling water for 1 minute 55 seconds, then shock them by plunging into cold water. Peel and chop in half.

Next, reheat the soup, then strain into a separate pan, either using a chinois (a posh, sieve essentially), or just a sieve, really pressing all of the liquid out. Season to taste.

Now just dress the bowl with all of the components and the pea shoots (which are now available from most supermarkets) – get creative, and try to make a little 'garden' ready for the soup to be poured over at the table ... Told you it's fancy!

PRAWN & CHILLI BISQUE WITH PRAWN TOASTS

This is another really tasty little number, and super easy to do. Serves 6

FOR THE BISQUE
KNOB OF BUTTER
25ML OLIVE OIL
4 SHALLOTS, DICED
2 GARLIC CLOVE, CRUSHED
1 CELERY STICK, DICED
2 CARROTS, FINELY CHOPPED
½ RED CHILLI, DESEEDED AND
    FINELY DICED
1 FENNEL BULB, FINELY CHOPPED
12 TIGER PRAWNS, SHELLS
    AND HEADS SEPARATED
200ML WHITE WINE
1 LITRE FISH STOCK
400G CAN CHOPPED TOMATOES

FOR THE TOASTS
SMALL BUNCH OF FLAT-LEAF
PARSLEY, PLUS EXTRA, CHOPPED,
    TO GARNISH
1 GARLIC CLOVE
JUICE OF 1 LEMON
6 CROSTINI
40G SESAME SEEDS
25ML OLIVE OIL
SALT AND FRESHLY GROUND
    BLACK PEPPER

Heat the butter and oil in a large pan and fry the shallots, garlic, celery, carrots, chilli and fennel over a medium heat until they begin to soften.

Once softened, add the prawn shells and heads and fry over a medium heat, until the shells turn deep pink. Add the wine, and scrape the bottom of the pan using a wooden spoon. Then add the fish stock and chopped tomatoes. Bring to the boil, and then reduce to a simmer for at least 1½ hours. The longer it's slowly simmered, the deeper the flavours will become. Try to allow the liquid to reduce by about one-third.

Blitz the contents of the pan using a hand-held electric blender, before passing through a fine sieve. You should be left with a dark orange soup that will taste bangarang!

Once strained through the sieve, return the soup to the pan, and simmer gently. Poach the raw prawns in the soup for around 4 minutes, or until opaque all the way through. Remove with a slotted spoon and reserve.

Place 6 of the prawns in a food processor with the parsley, garlic, lemon juice and seasoning. Spread the mixture on to the crostini, and sprinkle with sesame seeds. Heat the oil in a medium frying pan over a medium heat and fry the toasts, prawnside down for 2–3 minutes.

To serve, place the poached prawns and prawn toast in the bowl, with a sprinkle of chopped parsley, before adding the bisque.

BEEF CHEEK
& ALE PIE WITH
CHOCOLATE

Now I'm no Willy Wonka, but I always find beef cheek with a touch of chocolate to be a delight. Indeed, I know many a chilli con carne recipe that contains chocolate too. Serves 6

15ML VEGETABLE OIL
2 BEEF CHEEKS, SINEW REMOVED, AND CUT INTO 2CM CHUNKS
1 ONION, SLICED
1 CELERY STICK, SLICED
2 GARLIC CLOVES, FINELY CHOPPED
2 CARROTS, CHOPPED
500ML ALE OR STOUT
2 SPRIGS OF THYME
SPRIG OF ROSEMARY
1 BAY LEAF
50G DARK CHOCOLATE
15 X 25CM SHEET PUFF PASTRY (APPROXIMATELY 150G)
2 MEDIUM EGGS, BEATEN

Preheat the oven to 160°C/gas mark 3.

First off, heat the oil in a large, lidded flameproof casserole dish, and seal the meat on all sides over a high heat, until browned. Remove the meat from the dish using a slotted spoon and transfer to a plate.

Add the onion, celery and garlic to the dish, adding a little more oil if necessary, and cook until softened. Remove from the pan and add to the meat.

Finally, add the carrots and sauté for 6 minutes.

Whilst the pan is still over the heat, remove the carrots and add the ale to deglaze the pan. Scrape the bottom of the pan while it bubbles away. This will not only taste bangin' but will also save on washing up!

Place the meat and all the veg back into the dish with the herbs and 400ml water, place the lid on, and cook for around 3½ hours, or until the meat is tender.

When the beef is falling apart, remove the herbs and discard. Strain the cooking liquor into a small pan, skim off the fat, and bring to a boil, then simmer until reduced by half. Once it's reduced, lower the heat right down, and whisk in the dark chocolate. When the chocolate has melted, return the sauce to the casserole dish.

Increase the oven temperature to 200°C/gas mark 6.

Cut out the puff pastry to fit the top of the casserole dish and lay it over the top of the meat. Score a couple of lines through the middle of the pastry, brush with the beaten egg and bake for 30 minutes or until the puff pastry rises and is golden brown.

Serve it up family style with some creamy mash or maybe some of those lovely Dauphinoise (page 53)!

JIMMY'S SORREL PESTO

I love sorrel... it grows everywhere and has a distinct, tangy, almost kiwi fruit flavour and is vibrant green. Delicious stuff! Serves 4

600G TAGLIATELLE
A HANDFUL OF FRESH SORREL
    LEAVES
50G FLAKED ALMONDS, TOASTED
2 GARLIC CLOVES, CRUSHED
50ML GOOD-QUALITY OLIVE OIL
JUICE AND ZEST OF 1 LEMON
50G GRATED PARMESAN CHEESE

Bring a pan of water to the boil and blanch the tagliatelle (follow packet instructions, but it should take 8–11 minutes).

To make the pesto, place all the ingredients into a food processor and blitz.

Once the pasta is cooked, drain into a colander and divide it into warmed bowls, stir in the pesto and grub's up!

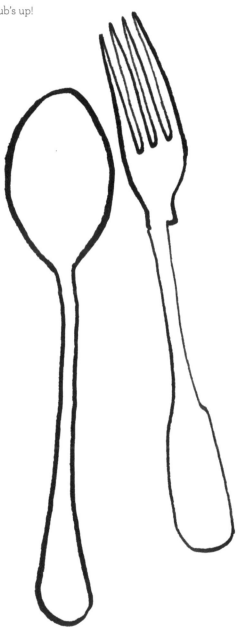

MOROCCAN CHICKEN & COUSCOUS

This can either be done as a main meal, or perhaps a salad as part of a barbie, or even as a great lunch to take to work! Couscous is one of those things that a lot of people find bland, but when done right, that couldn't be further from the truth! Give it a go! Serves 4

FOR THE CHICKEN
JUICE OF 1 LEMON
2 GARLIC CLOVES, CRUSHED
1 TEASPOON TAHINI PASTE
1 TABLESPOON CLEAR HONEY
2 TABLESPOONS OLIVE OIL
1 TABLESPOON CAYENNE PEPPER
1 TEASPOON PAPRIKA
1 TABLESPOON CUMIN
1 TEASPOON TURMERIC
½ TEASPOON GROUND CINNAMON
4 CHICKEN BREASTS

FOR THE COUSCOUS
1 COURGETTE, FINELY CHOPPED
1 RED PEPPER, DESEEDED AND
  FINELY CHOPPED
DRIZZLE OF OLIVE OIL
SALT AND FRESHLY GROUND
  BLACK PEPPER
200G COUSCOUS
½ RED ONION, DICED
50G SESAME SEEDS, TOASTED
JUICE AND ZEST OF 2 ORANGES
1 CHICKEN STOCK CUBE
1 TABLESPOON CUMIN
1 TABLESPOON CURRY POWDER
1 TEASPOON GROUND CINNAMON
BUNCH OF CORIANDER,
  FINELY CHOPPED
50G ALMONDS, TOASTED

Place all the chicken marinade ingredients into a large mixing bowl along with the chicken breasts, and leave to marinate in the fridge, overnight if possible.

For the couscous, preheat the oven to 180°C/gas mark 4. Place the courgette and red pepper into a roasting tray with a drizzle of olive oil, season and roast for about 15 minutes. These will add a lovely texture and colour to the couscous. Leave the oven on.

Place the couscous in a heatproof bowl and add all the remaining ingredients, apart from the toasted almonds, and mix thoroughly.

Boil the kettle and pour boiling water into the bowl until there is about double the volume of water to couscous. Cover with a tea towel for 5 minutes. After this time, give the couscous a good stir with your hand, rubbing the grains between your thumb and index finger to separate them.

The vegetables should be ready now (keep the oven on!), so stir them into the couscous along with the toasted almonds and set aside whilst you cook the chicken.

The chicken deserves to be cooked on a griddle pan! Heat the griddle pan over a high heat with a drizzle of olive oil and fry the chicken breasts for about 3 minutes on each side until clear char lines show. Transfer the chicken to the oven and roast for a further 10 minutes. Enjoy!

PORTOBELLO MUSHROOMS STUFFED WITH SPINACH, RICOTTA & CRISPY ONIONS

This is a lovely veggie snack that you can pair up with a nice side salad if you so wish. Serves 4

100G SPINACH
JUICE OF 1 LEMON
300G RICOTTA
4 PORTOBELLO MUSHROOMS
2 GARLIC CLOVES, CHOPPED
SALT AND FRESHLY GROUND
   BLACK PEPPER

FOR THE CRISPY ONIONS
50G CORNFLOUR
½ ONION, SLICED INTO RINGS
1 LITRE VEGETABLE OIL FOR
   DEEP FRYING

Preheat the oven to 180°C/gas mark 4.

Whizz up the spinach, lemon juice and ricotta in a blender until fully mixed.

Place the mushrooms, stalk side up, on a baking tray. Sprinkle the garlic into the mushrooms, then add a good dollop of the ricotta and spinach mix, season and bake for 15 minutes.

For the crispy onions, place the cornflour in a shallow dish. Coat the onion rings in the cornflour. Heat the oil in a deep pan to 160°C (check with a kitchen thermometer or see page 22) and fry the onions until they begin to turn a golden colour and crisp up.

Sit the onions on top of the mushrooms and there you go!

LAMBS' KIDNEYS WITH GARLIC

This dish brings back fond memories of watching football Italia with my dad on a Sunday after church. The better the quality of the lamb, the much better and cleaner the kidney will taste, so be sure to buy these from a good butcher who knows where his meat is from, and ask him nicely to remove the gristle for you. Serves 4

100G LARDONS
30ML OLIVE OIL
KNOB OF BUTTER
2 BANANA SHALLOTS, FINELY
   CHOPPED
1 GARLIC CLOVE, FINELY
   CHOPPED
1 CELERY STICK, FINELY
   CHOPPED
SPRIGS OF THYME AND ROSEMARY,
   LEAVES FINELY CHOPPED
100G BUTTON MUSHROOMS
6 LAMBS' KIDNEYS, HALVED
120ML RED WINE
1 BAY LEAF
CRUSTY BREAD, TO SERVE

Place the lardons in a medium non-stick frying pan with the oil and butter and fry over a high heat until crispy, then transfer to a plate and set aside. Next, add the shallots, garlic, celery and the chopped thyme and rosemary, and cook over a medium heat for around 5 minutes before adding the mushrooms for a further 2 minutes, then transfer to the plate.

Finally, add the lambs' kidneys to the pan, with a little more butter if necessary, and cook for 3 minutes on each side, before adding the red wine and deglazing the pan. Add the bay leaf and the reserved ingredients and cook for another 2 minutes before serving it up with some crusty bread. A quick and simple delight!

ASPARAGUS, PEA & PARMESAN RISOTTO

This dish is a perfect way to enjoy the spring season ... British asparagus, arguably the best in the world, blooms around May, along with spring peas and lots of other treats, so this is a great homage to the beginning of the season! Serves 4

ABOUT 1.5 LITRES VEGETABLE
    STOCK
50G BUTTER
DRIZZLE OF OLIVE OIL
1½ ONIONS, FINELY DICED
1 CELERY STICK, FINELY DICED
1 CARROT, PEELED AND
    FINELY DICED
2 GARLIC CLOVES, CRUSHED
400G RISOTTO/ARBORIO RICE
175ML WHITE WINE
200G FROZEN PEAS
BUNCH OF PARSLEY, CHOPPED
100G GRATED PARMESAN
JUICE OF 1 LEMON
SALT AND FRESHLY GROUND
    BLACK PEPPER
8 ASPARAGUS SPEARS

Place the stock in a large saucepan and keep it warm over a low heat, ready to ladle into the risotto.

For the risotto, heat the butter and oil in a large pan over a medium heat and fry the onions, celery, carrot and garlic for 5 minutes. Add the risotto rice, stirring it continuously for 5 minutes.

Add the white wine to the pan and continue stirring, allowing the rice to soak up all the wine.

Add a ladleful of hot stock at a time to the risotto pan and continue stirring, so that the rice absorbs the moisture before you add another ladle of stock. Continue this process over a low heat for about 15 minutes, then add the peas, parsley and Parmesan to the pan, and continue stirring for a further 5 minutes, adding more stock. After this time, taste the rice to check it's cooked and season with salt and black pepper and add the lemon juice.

For the asparagus spears, heat a drizzle of olive oil in a griddle pan over a high heat and cook the asparagus for about 3 minutes.

Serve the risotto in warmed bowls, with 2 asparagus spears on top of each bowl!

PRAWN & CHORIZO LINGUINE

This used to be one of my go to dinners when I was a broker. If it had been a late one and I just got back from work, this could be rustled up in no time ... 20 minutes from kitchen to plate! Serves 2

250G LINGUINE
SPLASH OLIVE OIL
½ RED ONION FINELY DICED
2 CLOVE GARLIC
1 SWEET RED PEPPER,
   FINELY DICED
200G PEELED PRAWNS
200G FRESH, CHERRY TOMATOES,
   HALVED
50G CHORIZO, CUT IN TO
   1CM CUBES
100ML WHITE WINE
½ BUNCH BASIL LEAVES TORN
SALT AND FRESHLY GROUND
   BLACK PEPPER

Place a large pan of boiling water on a high heat with some salt, and bring to the boil.

Add the linguine and follow cooking instructions on the packet (usually about 8 minutes), before draining and setting aside to serve.

For the sauce, place the olive oil, red onion, garlic, and red pepper in a saucepan over a medium heat and cook for 4-5 minutes, until all the veg begins to soften.

Add the prawns, cherry tomatoes and chorizo, and fry for one minute, before adding the white wine. Simmer for a couple of minutes until the wine has reduced by two thirds and the prawns have cooked, about another 5 minutes.

Take the pan off the heat, and add the torn basil and salt and pepper before serving ... bosh!

INDEX